Praise for
SUCCEEDING with SENIOR MANAGEMENT

"Michael Campbell has written the classic survival manual for the project manager. He convincingly shows how factors external to the project team have a major impact on success, providing proven prescriptions on how to handle relationships with sponsors, functional managers, and future users. Should be required reading for project managers everywhere."

—Dr. Gary L. Richardson
PMI Professor of Project Management, University of Houston

"Most complex projects that fail do so because the organization doesn't understand how to structure and support a project, not because the project manager doesn't know how to manage the project plan. Michael Campbell lays out a roadmap for managing the broader project environment and sponsorship, which is the most important indicator of ultimate project success. This book is required reading for managing projects with significant business dependencies."

—Stephen Schwarz
Chief Operating Officer, ABS Nautical Systems

"Michael Campbell has worked in the Project Management weeds, and he's worked in the executive suites. He has bridged the gap with this book! As I read it, I felt like I was having a conversation with the leadership team and the project manager, hearing both sides of the conversation. One of our customers told me 'I need you to teach our Project Managers to think like leadership, because our presentations are not giving them what they need.' If I had *Succeeding with Senior Management: Getting the Right Support at the Right Time for Your Project* at the time, it would have been an easy task to change their thinking. I left reading the book feeling uplifted."

—Henry B. "Skeeter" Lieberum
President, Global Dynamic Consulting

"Michael Campbell has put aside all the theories and has developed a practical guide for project managers on how to navigate the treacherous waters of the politics of successfully performing projects. Finally, a book that deals with the underlying currents that can cause projects to either crash or reach their desired destination. Tired of getting blindsided by factors beyond your control? Read this book to learn how to take better control of your, and your projects', destiny.

—Doug Boebinger, PMP
President & CEO of Integrated Process Developers, Inc.

"In this book, Michael Campbell broaches the question that ought to be on project managers' minds: 'How do I work with and influence the key executive stakeholders and sponsors to my work?' This isn't taught in most business schools or *PMBOK Guide®*. Nobody tells us what sponsors need or want. But so many projects have a perception of failure simply because of broken sponsor relationships. Mr. Campbell draws upon current research and his wealth of experience to answer this key question."

—William Dannenmaier
CEO/Project Management/Training
BlackBox Migrations, LLC

"Michael Campbell's grasp of difficult subjects and his ability to present solutions with relative ease is recognized among the project management community worldwide. He continues to make a valuable contribution, with innovative solutions, to his profession through consulting, publishing books, and making presentations at various platforms including conferences."

—Terry Minhas
Senior Vice President, External Operations
Project Management Institute, Houston

SUCCEEDING
with
SENIOR
MANAGEMENT

G. MICHAEL CAMPBELL, PMP

SUCCEEDING
with
SENIOR
MANAGEMENT

GETTING THE RIGHT SUPPORT AT THE
RIGHT TIME FOR YOUR PROJECT

HarperCollins
Leadership

An Imprint of HarperCollins

Published by HarperCollins Leadership, an imprint of HarperCollins Focus LLC, 501 Nelson Place, Nashville, TN 37214, USA.

Any internet addresses, phone numbers, or company or product information printed in this book are offered as a resource and are not intended in any way to be or to imply an endorsement by HarperCollins Leadership, nor does HarperCollins Leadership vouch for the existence, content, or services of these sites, phone numbers, companies, or products beyond the life of this book.

ISBN 978-1-4002-5236-7 (TP)
ISBN 978-0-8144-3852-7 (eBook)

HarperCollins Publishers, Macken House, 39/40 Mayor Street Upper, Dublin 1, D01 C9W8, Ireland (https://www.harpercollins.com)

Library of Congress Cataloging-in-Publication Data

Names: Campbell, G. Michael, 1948- author.
Title: Succeeding with senior management : getting the right support at the
   right time for your project / G. Michael Campbell, PMP.
Description: New York, NY : AMACOM, [2017] | Includes index.
Identifiers: LCCN 2017005309 (print) | LCCN 2017022224 (ebook) | ISBN
   9780814438527 (E-book) | ISBN 9780814438503 (pbk.)
Subjects: LCSH: Project management.
Classification: LCC HD69.P75 (ebook) | LCC HD69.P75 C36423 2017 (print) | DDC
   658.4/04—dc23
LC record available at https://lccn.loc.gov/2017005309

This book is dedicated to all those project managers who have struggled to get the attention and support from their sponsor needed to make their project a success. I hope this book gives you a practical roadmap. I would love to hear your comments through book reviews on Amazon and I promise to make every effort respond to you. Best wishes to all of you operating within the triple constraint!

ACKNOWLEDGMENTS

I would like to thank Tim Burgard for believing in this book and providing guidance and direction. I have appreciated the opportunity to work with such a terrific editor and organization.

To Miranda Pennington and all those at Neuwirth & Associates who worked to helped make this book polished and professional.

There are so many people to thank for their ability to teach me how to become better at managing my projects, especially Stephen Schwarz, Chuck Brown, Leslie Warren, Henry "Skeeter" Lieberum, Marc Edwards, Tim Probert, Jack Moore, John Bartos, Dave Feineman and Terry Minhas.

To my wife, Molly, who continues to support my dreams. Her love and the love of my family remains the foundation of my life.

And to you, the readers, who have purchased this book. I understand how important projects are to your personal and professional success. I feel honored that you believe I can teach you a little something in your quest to become a better project manager.

CONTENTS

1

Understanding the Facts of Life for Executives

EVERY PROJECT MANAGER who has run a project knows that the support of senior management is a critical factor in delivering a successful project—and honestly does not know how to get it. There are great books out there on running a project, from the *PMBOK (Project Management Body of Knowledge)*, to countless others ranging from the *Idiot's/Dummies'* guides with practical advice to the 1,200-page tomes like that of project management guru Dr. Harold Kerzner on every detail a project manager could imagine. Again, none of these books can help project managers plan the engagement with senior management—or tell them how to get the support they need when only senior managers can address the issues facing a project.

So if there is an obvious need, why haven't any books been written? I believe part of the answer lies in the nature of project management itself. Project managers think, as the name implies, like managers as they manage their Work Breakdown Structure, schedule, and budget. Senior management generally thinks more strategically and is really not interested in the details of the projects they sponsor.

One senior executive told me that the status report from his project manager was, in his words, "death by details!"

Therefore, sponsors and project managers don't speak the same language, nor do they approach the execution of a project the same way. For example, most leaders ponder long and hard over whether a project should be undertaken and whether the reward is worth the investment. From their strategic perspective, the capital being invested in any given project could have been used in other ways to make the company money, but they determined that this project was the right move, and so they placed their bet. Once they have sifted through all the options and have made the decision to go ahead, they believe their work is largely done. They assign the project to a project manager and expect that person to return when the project is completed—with occasional reports submitted along the way. The only senior manager who is still interested in the project, even though it is often a remote interest, is the executive named as the sponsor.

Project managers, however, are persons whose predisposition is to view a project as a tactical implementation. Therefore, they are often not well equipped to engage with senior management since they tend to focus on tasks and activities and not on the strategic business outcomes that are the focus of senior management. In that respect, they are very similar to middle managers who suffer from the same lack of ability to communicate and engage with their senior executives.

The goal of this book is to provide you, as a project manager, with a clear set of principles, as well as a blueprint for engaging with senior management to get the support you need when you need it.

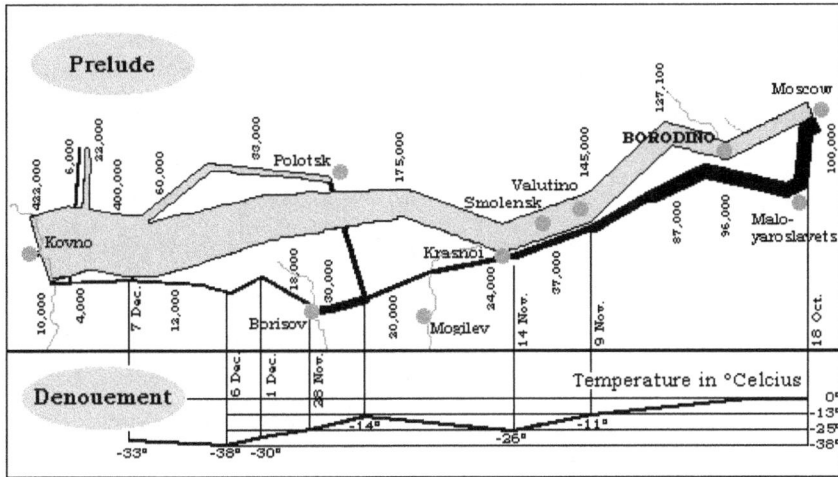

Figure 1.1: 1869 Chart by Charles Joseph Minard

Leadership's Traditional Role in a Project as Illustrated by Napoleon's March on Moscow

See Figure 1.1. The size of the bar indicates the relative strength of the French army during the march on Moscow, starting with more than 400,000 soldiers when they crossed the frontier from Poland. The dots represent major battles during the advance and the retreat. The black bar shows the dwindling French army during the retreat. It is remarkable to note that the army had shrunk to only 100,000 as they left Moscow. By the time they crossed back into Poland, just under 10,000 had survived. The lower portion of the map shows the temperature in degrees Celsius during the retreat, indicating the temperature of –38°C at the end. This is the place where the Celsius and Fahrenheit come together: It truly was a cold day in hell for the French army.

Like Napoleon's campaign against Russia, projects often start with great fanfare and all manner of support from everyone involved. Then battles—in projects we call them issues—occur as the project progresses, and support begins to dwindle. If project managers do not do a good job of managing expectations, engaging in change management, and providing robust communications, the entire project can be either rejected or ignored by the stakeholders. Worst of all, when the project is finally finished, almost no one in the leadership team, including the sponsor, even remembers there was a project. And if they do remember, they remember only the issues. How can we prevent this from happening to our projects? The secret to handling executives is what this book is all about. My perspective throughout much of the book will be related to publicly traded companies. However, I have worked in large nonprofits, such as the American Cancer Society, and most of what I will cover is true there as well.

Why Is Managing Executives So Difficult?

First of all, as project managers, we have to understand the environment these executives live in from day to day. As senior management, the leadership must manage two important workstreams simultaneously.

Daily Operational Performance

See Figure 1.2. On the one hand, there are all the elements required to succeed in operational performance. The operational priorities are:

- Constant pressure on profit and loss
- Minimizing headcount as much as possible
- Increasing productivity to do more with less
- Improving efficiency to drive waste out of the processes

These subjects are the topics, at a high level, that CEOs, CFOs, and others must be prepared to discuss during quarterly conference calls with Wall Street and their own Board of Directors.

Daily Operational Performance

Planning for Future Performance

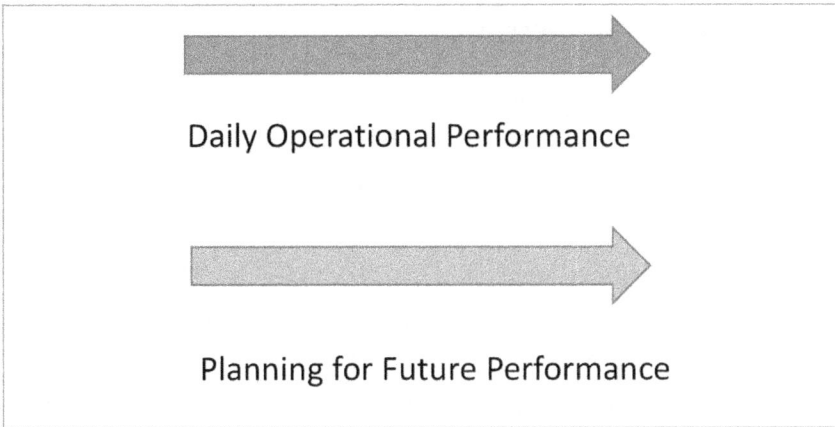

Figure 1.2: Dual Tracks That Executives Must Navigate

On the other hand, two major considerations come from a company's customers and competitors:

1. Provide lower prices.
2. Deliver better service.

Customers are constantly demanding lower prices and want better products and services for those lower prices. All executives know that the company's competitors are working hard to take customers away if the company fails to deliver on these two key demands.

Planning for Future Performance

A company's customers and competitors also drive a second priority: the need to address the needs of customers in the future. And that is where we usually come into the picture.

Projects Meet a Business Need

Projects are usually begun to address one or more demands. See Figure 1.3.

The drivers might be:

- A market demand to expand the production of products
- An organizational need to train people with new skills
- A specific request from a key customer
- A legal requirement from the government or regulatory body

Projects and programs may have a variety of outcomes in the forecast, but one constant is the same: the need to improve performance in the future. The sponsor is the person tasked by the executive to deliver on the business benefits. The project manager is the person who takes overall responsibility for coordinating a project, regardless of its size, and for making sure the desired end result is achieved on time and within budget. That is why it is so critical that the sponsor and project manager work together closely.

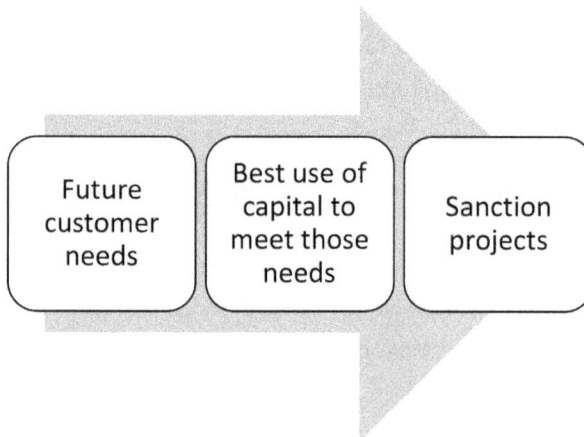

Future customer needs | Best use of capital to meet those needs | Sanction projects

Figure 1.3: Process for Sanctioning Projects

The whole plan for future performance starts with a discussion about what the leadership team believes the customers will want in the future. They must address the following questions regardless of whether the customers' needs are simply incremental or call for a true step change:

One executive told me that in discussing new products and services, management must have answers to these four questions:

1. Why do we believe that customers will pay us money for this new product or service?
2. Do we believe that we can successfully deliver this new product or service?
3. Can we manage the risks that may be involved in delivering this new product or service?
4. Do we have confidence that we can get the right return on investment once we turn over this new product or service to operations?

As you can imagine, the discussion is long and hard because the answers to all these questions are based on various assumptions. If another executive challenges those assumptions, the individual proposing the new product or service must be prepared to defend them. Obviously, there are no guarantees. In essence, the leadership team is really coming to a consensus about where to place their bets. And their bets usually involve large amounts of money!

Now add the fact that the company either can or is willing to spend only a limited amount of capital on these future initiatives. Once consensus is reached, the leadership team will decide which initiatives are sanctioned and become projects.

The crazy reality is that once the decisions are made, most of the executives no longer think about a particular project except one—the one who was named sponsor and is accountable for delivering the initiative.

Politics and Perception

Another fact of life for you to understand is the political arena your sponsor operates within. The higher a person gets to the top of the organization chart, the more competition there is for the next promotion because there are so few positions to move into. And don't forget that at this level, every company has a suite full of A-type personalities who are aggressive as well as assertive.

> Warren Buffet once observed that there are two rules in corporate business: "The first rule is not to lose. The second rule is not to forget the first rule."

That environment poses real hazards to your sponsor. He or she must appear to be in control of their project. Perception is a powerful force at this level. If the sponsor is perceived as weak or out of control, there will be a political price to pay. You must recognize that if your project appears out of control or failing, your sponsor will begin to distance themselves from you and the project. They cannot afford the price politically with their peers.

Once the project is sanctioned, that is the point where we, as project managers, enter the picture. We are not privy to all the discussions that occurred up to that point, but when we get to Chapter 3, I'll tell you how to learn more about what happened during these deliberations.

If the project manager understands the business requirements that are driving the project, the project will succeed. If not, it won't. In the long term, the project will be judged not only on how well it met the targeted objectives but also by whether it achieved its overall business objectives and the anticipated business value the project was supposed to capture. The project manager must work with the sponsor closely to seek regular feedback in order to ensure that the project, as currently defined, still achieves the business objectives. Several things may change during the course of a project, such as:

- Business conditions
- Company objectives
- Management personnel
- Relative priorities
- Risk factors that materialize requiring intervention to handle them

Often your sponsor will recognize these changes before you do. Therefore, keep this in mind when you talk with your sponsor about the project. Don't focus just on the tactical performance of the project, but utilize your sponsor to keep the strategic purpose in mind as well.

All project managers must understand one other fact in the constant tug-of-war between operational performance and future performance: The day-to-day will always win. How that will impact your project will depend on several factors, but all project managers must assess how this fact of life could impact their projects and must capture those risks and their mitigation strategies in their risk register.

One More Consideration

The Project Management Institute (PMI) gathered data as part of their *Pulse of the Profession® In-Depth Report* in 2014 and discovered some very interesting disconnects between sponsors and project managers. Here are the results in key areas related to projects:

- Motivating the project team:
  - 34% of project managers say that sponsors frequently seek to motivate the team.
  - 82% of sponsors say they motivate the team frequently.
  - That is a 48% gap in perception.

- Active listening:
  - 42% of project managers say sponsors actively listen frequently.
  - 88% of sponsors say they actively listen frequently.
  - That is a 46% gap in perception.

- Communication:
  - 47% of project managers perceive that the sponsor frequently communicates effectively.
  - 92% of sponsors report communicating frequently and effectively.
  - That is a 45% gap in perception.

- Managing change during implementation:
  - 37% of project managers observe that sponsors manage change effectively.
  - 82% of sponsors claim that they manage change effectively.
  - That is a 45% gap in perception.

It should be obvious that project managers and their sponsors have very different perceptions related to the effectiveness of project sponsors.

The purpose of this chapter was to help you understand why you may have difficulties in receiving the support you need from your sponsor when you need it. The remaining chapters will explore how you can change that dynamic and get the right support at the right time for your project.

Points to Remember

- Understand the facts of life for executives.
- Recognize the difficulties in keeping their attention during a project.
- Keep the focus on business results.

2

Preparing the Leadership

IN CHAPTER 1, we looked at the reason managing leadership is so difficult. We also noted the disconnect regarding leadership involvement between executives and the project managers who report to them. So the project manager must address the question, "Why is executive leadership so important to the success of a project?" The simple answer is that people respond to the agenda that their "boss" feels is important. And how do they determine what is important to the boss? They read the signals—they notice what the boss talks about and pays attention to over time. If you consider your own situation, you probably recognize this tendency in your own experience.

How Involved Should the Leadership Be?

Although the leadership will seldom have the time or interest to be "in on the details" concerning particular activities and tasks, it will be important for the project manager to communicate specific roles and responsibilities for them. The project manager must work with the sponsor to communicate to the leadership team that, at certain times during the project, he will call upon them to participate actively and deliver messages or intervene when difficulties occur. For example, if you need a leader to give an important message to the organization about expecting commitment from people for the project, she should be willing to do that.

Therefore, the project manager must develop a detailed communications plan that highlights to the sponsor and others in leadership when they will be called on to send certain messages or participate in certain activities and that they are key to the success of the project. In my experience, leaders are often more than willing to communicate to the organization if they understand how they can contribute and why it is important for the message to come from them personally.

If you are a strong communicator, this will usually mean that you (or, if you are not a strong communicator, someone from the project team) will be required to craft the message or at least provide a draft that the executive can deliver.

MANAGING RISK

In most cases, a company leader will want to review and edit the message so that it sounds more like the way she would deliver it. There's nothing wrong with that, as long as the basic idea stays intact. If the leader (or corporate communications) begins to edit the communication in such a way that it loses the core meaning, you may need to do a better job of explaining what you are trying to accomplish and educate her on the risks and possible consequences involved in straying from the way you've developed the content.

If there is a communication specialist in the project team to develop the messages, you may need to get this person involved in the conversation. A specialist may have a better chance of explaining the intent of the wording and approach as drafted, especially if he drafted it.

Also, many project managers deal with multiple layers of management during the course of planning and executing their projects. Mid-level managers are notoriously difficult to deal with, but we need them. Why must the project manager work with them? The reason is fairly classic: They are the people who supervise most of the work done in the company. Remember the discussion in the previous chapter about operations and strategic perspective? These managers focus only on the operational side, and your project has a different agenda. If they do not understand or see visible evidence of commitment from the senior managers, they may feel that their compliance is optional, not mandatory. Navigating these political waters will require the help of senior executives at times. Occasionally, some of these midlevel managers may even challenge the project, probably as much to test the commitment of the executive team as to question some of the business decisions being made. It is beyond the capability of most project managers to address a challenge from this group.

Choosing a Project Champion

The idea of having an executive sponsor has been around for a long time. There are not going to be a lot of details on that role here because it has been covered very well in other books, as well as in the *Project Management Book of Knowledge (PMBOK)*. However, as most of us who have managed projects for any length of time recognize, it is often very difficult to keep sponsors engaged throughout a long project so that they are ready to help you at key junctures in the project. That is why I believe it is important to turn to the additional role of project champion. In my experience, the best candidate for champion has some critical characteristics that will help you make a project successful:

- First and foremost, they are trusted explicitly by the sponsor and are able to provide that executive with clear and unambiguous information about the project. Such knowledge can be good news or bad news but can also be requests for help. Most of the time, champions report to the sponsor and, as a result, often have easier access to her than the project manager.
- Secondly, they have broad understanding of the various segments of the business that are impacted by the project. Our most successful champions are usually people at the director level who have handled operational assignments in various parts of the organization.
- They act as the chair of the Working Committee (which I will describe in detail later) and lead that group since they will often be successful in steering through political waters.
- They work with the sponsor on cross-functional issues. Each of the departments represented in the project may have different executives and managers, and someone will have to help you navigate the issues and come to a resolution.

As you can see, the sponsor and champion can help you in many ways.

Dangerous Assumptions Made by Operations

Another role that you will need your sponsor and champion to assume is educating the operations group about their role in the project.

Operations makes three assumptions that must be corrected:

1. Operations assumes that the project owns the preparation for implementation. In fact, the operations team must take ownership of the implementation.
2. Operations will underestimate the complexity and difficulty of getting ready for the project deliverables. Most of my

projects have been new systems or applications, and operations usually thinks that they are simply plug-and-play like the latest video game. It is just not true.

3. Operations does not appreciate the amount of time required to create alignment within the work processes.

All of these assumptions will require the help of the sponsor and/or champion to address. One of those ways may be in communications. Indeed, as project manager, I may typically draft the initial communications, such as e-mails, announcements, and presentations, that the sponsor and champion make to the organization. However, it is crucially important that these critical communications come from them and not from me as the project manager. When we look at the stakeholder analysis in Chapter 6, one of the key questions will be who should deliver the message? In most cases of communication outside the project team, the communication should be delivered by either the sponsor or the champion—but more about that later.

After securing the champion, I try to work with him to find the right people to fill a Working Committee team.

Developing a Working Committee and Working Groups

I believe the successful project manager will treat members of the Working Committee as a critical extension of her project team. There are several considerations in pulling together a working committee and the various working groups. As stated earlier, the task is to identify and nominate the best key people the company has to offer.

Unfortunately, these same people are often asked to take on these types of roles because they are outstanding and respected. I have often had to explain to my sponsor that a key indication of stakeholder leadership support is their willingness to provide these people for work on the project. There is a real risk in this strategy. In pursuing it, I have to make sure I am not being lured into taking people because they are "available." As you will soon discover, if you haven't already, there is usually a reason no one wants them working on their projects.

> **The greatest difference between a Working Committee and a working group is that the Working Committee should remain intact throughout the project, whereas a working group is given a specific issue or problem to solve and then is disbanded.**

It is very important to draw on the various departments or groups that will be impacted by the changes the project will force on them when it is finished. The basic mandate for the Working Committee is to consider various options that have been presented from the project team and to make decisions about which options should be implemented.

Risk Management

In a project that I led to implement a customer relationship management (CRM) system, I had a project that affected nearly every department in the company, which sold hospital equipment and supplies. To provide some background, a CRM system is a technology that allows companies to manage and analyze the customer relationship with the goal of improving customer service and producing more revenue. Therefore, my project needed key players from sales, marketing, information technology, accounting, manufacturing, and procurement. In effect, each of these people represented a "constituency" within the company, and they needed to be chosen with that role in mind. As the project team explored ways to implement the CRM solution, I asked the Working Committee members to remember that they were to involve these

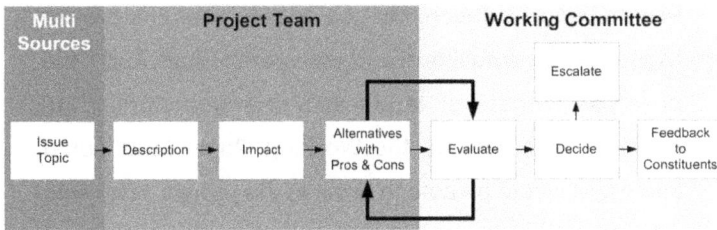

Figure 2.1: Process for Business Process Change

key constituents routinely in the discussions about changes affecting the business.

Communications and the Working Committee

One of the key questions some of the members of the Working Committee had was, "Why does this group have a role in communications during a project?" And that was a good question. Here was the answer. They were the vehicle—the eyes, ears, and voice—for keeping people informed about what the project was doing and for providing the project team with feedback on concerns in operations about what we are doing. The working committee members were going to be asked to follow a process for decision making that involved their constituency.

During the project, I asked for and received agreement from the Working Committee members that before any key decision was made related to changes the project might make, the Working Committee would conduct discussions with their constituency and poll them on their thoughts and concerns (see Figure 2.1).

The information the committee members received was to be brought back to the project team for discussion before a decision was made. Any concerns could then be addressed, and the team could base their decision on the best way to get the job done for the business, not on the best technical solution. My goal was to keep the project aligned with the business and commercial side. And if the business climate or landscape changed during the course of the project, the Working Committee would know and would be able to provide the project team with a fair warning.

Be aware that some Working Committee members will not hold discussions with or inform their constituents and will attempt to make the decisions on their own. That really defeats the purpose of a Working Committee. To prevent this, I often develop independent relationships with other people within the various constituencies. I regularly seek them out to test what they are hearing from their Working Committee member and how knowledgeable they are about the project. That has worked well for me, and I have been able to specifically address my concerns with any Working Committee members who were not communicating well, citing specific examples.

The beauty of this arrangement is that the Working Committee spreads the news about what is going on in the project. And after decisions are made, the Working Committee members are in a position to defend their decisions later if their constituency objects to any of them. Ultimately, the most effective communication vehicle for serious messages come from people within the Working Committee when the groups impacted by the project both trust the committee and believe that it is looking out for their interests.

Working Groups

Working groups are often a subset of the Working Committee, but they usually include other members with specific knowledge or

Working Committee	Working Group
• Responsible for recommendations on all business aspects of the project	• Responsible for a recommendation on one problem or issue
• Represent the functions impacted by the project	• Represent only the function(s) impacted by a problem or issue
• Part of the project for the entire duration	• Disbanded once a recommendation is accepted

Figure 2.2: Working Committee and Working Groups

expertise. See Figure 2.2. Working groups will typically handle two types of issues, that is, when the problem:

▪ Affects only a small group
▪ Uncovers a bad business practice that is beyond the scope of the project

Let's take a look at each of these situations to illustrate them.

One example of issue 1 was when the project team ran into a conflict between the sales department and the accounting and invoicing departments. The issue was the relative importance of entering accurate information into the CRM. The position the sales department took was that they wanted to spend their time driving sales and identifying potential sales opportunities. They did not want to enter data into a computer. They saw such tasks as relatively unimportant, even as they recognized that accurate information could help them identify additional opportunities. On the other side of the equation was the accounting and invoicing group, who had to have accurate data and information to complete the company's financial reporting, not to mention to receive timely payment from customers. They complained that, under the "old" way, they spent entirely too much time correcting input errors and conducting reconciliations.

In a situation like this one, the unaffected members of the Working Committee did not really need to be in on all the detailed aspects of this discussion, so Rod, the project manager, created a working group that included the representatives from sales and accounting, as well as four other key individuals. Their group was charged with exploring the options and coming back to the full Working Committee with two recommendations on:

- The minimum information required for the end-to-end process to be effective
- Who would do the data entry into the CRM and why

The project manager also requested the supporting rationale for the two recommendations. It was a way to get the working group to think through how they would explain the decisions. (Coincidentally, the project manager had the content of the communications surrounding the decision!)

You can begin to see the value of this approach for communicating the decisions the project is making related to the question of data entry. Later on, if the accounting people grumbled about the lack of information or the sales team complained about entering orders into the CRM system, they could be reminded that their peers made the decision. It was endorsed by the full Working Committee and sanctioned by senior management. That was a powerful message and could be delivered by the right people who have credibility with each group.

Second, projects often uncover bad business practices that are really out of scope for the project. As an example in our case study, the project team learned that one of the key problems in moving contracts from sales to manufacturing for order scheduling was the length of time the legal department took to review contracts. It was pretty clear that this team should not take on a potential process problem within the legal department. Therefore, the project manager went to the champion and encouraged the organization of a working group consisting of sales, legal, and manufacturing to deal with this issue. This action meant that the issue was immediately taken out of the Working Committee and the project team's scope of work. The champion was now responsible for getting that piece of work completed. And it had a major benefit in solving a serious business problem that was affecting customer responsiveness.

In both of these situations, the Working Committee and the working groups acted as the primary communication vehicles related to the problems the project was seeking to solve, as well as the decisions that were being made. That is not to say that direct communications informing key stakeholders were no longer needed: Any project manager must still do the job of ensuring that multiple lines of communication remain open. However, the job of communication is made much easier by using this approach.

Finally, you must realize that the biggest potential obstacle to the successful implementation of project deliverables is the middle management layer within the company. If you think about it, it makes perfect sense: Middle managers are critical linchpins in the organization. You must keep these managers well informed so that you are informed and aware of possible concerns they have regarding your project. The Working Committee members can be the perfectly suited people to communicate with these managers. If the project manager in this case study was hearing concerns about the project from some of the manufacturing supervisors, who better to go with her to talk with them than the manufacturing representative from the Working Committee? We'll talk more about how to work with them and how to craft the messages when we get to the communications plan in Chapter 10. And in Chapter 11 we will look at how to use the communication plan to address potential project risks.

Points to Remember

- Determine how involved the management needs to be in your project.
- Provide the appropriate leaders with a script on when you will call on them.
- Develop a Working Committee to make the business decisions related to the project.
- Identify a champion who can lead the Working Committee and also has the credibility to engage the leadership when their presence is required.

3

Questions Every Project Manager Really Needs Answered

OFTEN THE PROBLEM between project managers and their sponsors starts right at the beginning. That is why I am encouraging you to work with your sponsor to get the answers to the questions posed in this chapter. Keep in mind that the sponsor:

- May not have the answer but can help you find someone who does have that answer.
- Can facilitate a meeting with key stakeholders who would often be difficult for you to access on your own.

A project manager may have a contract or a Charter, but these documents do not really answer some critical questions that you, as project manager, need the answers to. Why? As one example, if you are reviewing a contract, remember its source and context. This document was written by an attorney or by multiple attorneys and uses their language and context. While it can be helpful in understanding some high-level considerations such as deliverables, many other pieces are missing.

In my experience in doing projects over the years, I have learned that there is seldom just one technical way to fix an issue or address a problem. So how do we choose the best solution to the problem? Most of the time, the choice is what we, as project managers, or our team technical leads believe is the best technical solution. While that sounds simple and logical, we can find that we picked the answer that was not what our sponsor was looking for. Let me provide an example from my experience.

Earlier in my career, before I learned to ask these questions, I was in charge of implementing a new automation system for my client's on-shore oil fields across North America. The desire of my sponsor, as expressed to me, was to create a system that provided data faster to the central command centers that monitored and operated the fields. The mistake I made was not asking my sponsor to define what he meant when he used the term "faster." You can probably already guess what happened. My team and I worked very hard and brought the system upgrade online with speeds that were 20% faster than before. We all congratulated ourselves with high-fives all around. However, all that was short-lived. When I reported our success to the sponsor, that was when I learned that, in his mind, *faster* meant that the data would be near real-time, which was more than 50% faster than the old system. Therefore, in his mind, the project was really a business failure even though I could claim it as a technical success.

Could we have given him a system that was nearly real-time? Absolutely, but not with the budget and schedule we had been given. If I had asked the questions you will read in the following pages, I would have realized that we—the sponsor and project manager—were not on the same page. I could have explained that the system he envisioned could be delivered but would have required a major retrofit of hardware in many of the fields, plus an upgrade in the connectivity components. The project would have easily cost twice what our budget was and at least an additional year. My guess is that had I understood his definition of *faster* and explained what would be required to make it happen, he would have been quite pleased with a 20% increase in speed. I don't think there would have been an appetite for that much more money and time.

If my sponsor and I were aligned in the definition of *faster*, I believe the project would have been perceived as a business success as well as a technical success.

So what are the questions that help you get inside the head of your sponsor? Here are the questions that can provide you with crucial background that will allow you to be aligned with your sponsor.

What Is Broken or Not Working as Expected?

In uncovering the answer to this question, think about the classic questions for inquiry:

- Who is impacted or affected?
- How does this impact the business?
  - What are your role and responsibilities as sponsor?
  - What are the role and responsibilities of those who report to you?
- How frequently does this situation occur?
- What would you like to be able to do?
- What constraints, assumptions, and complexities exist?

Let's look at each of these questions as a way to ensure that we understand the scope of the project. See Figure 3.1.

Who Is Impacted or Affected?

The answer to this question is crucial to help us understand who the key stakeholders are for our project. This answer is probably why the

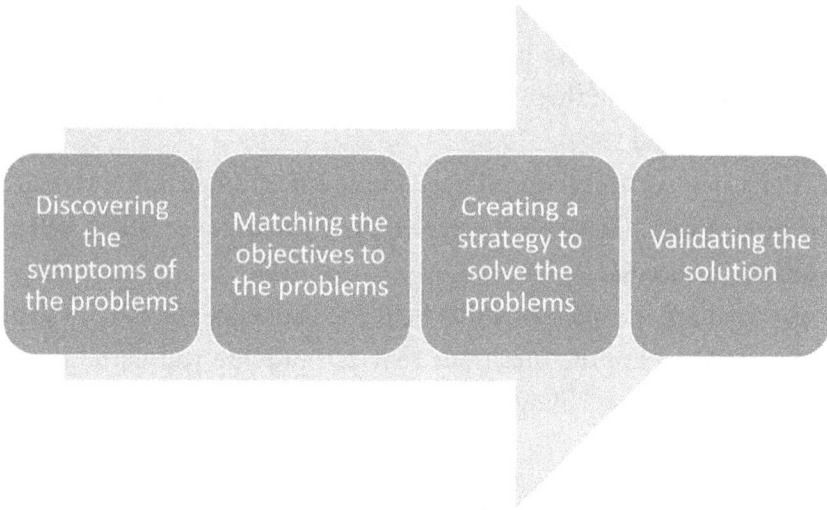

Figure 3.1: Understanding the Context

executive who became your sponsor is overseeing the project. Other key stakeholders may not have any decision-making role in the project, but they may have veto power over some portions of it. Their satisfaction with the solution will be a significant opinion in whether the project is ultimately viewed as a success. In uncovering the answer here, try to get as specific or as granular as possible.

In a project for an SAP (systems applications and products) upgrade, the project was moving along well until SAP announced that the company was releasing an upgraded module for procurement. As you can imagine, the supply chain people wanted to increase the scope of the project to include this module.

In briefing the sponsor and then the Steering Committee, the project team explained what the change in scope would mean. One of the impacts was to the accounting department. Just understanding that it impacts the accounting department was not going to be sufficient. What the accounting department explained to us and then to the Steering Committee was that the impact was on their year-end ability to close the books. They were very worried about trying to complete their work before the system had been stabilized.

The Steering Committee understood the concern and decided to delay the supply chain module and complete it as part of a new phase in the second quarter of the following year.

Please consider that, when you are getting your answers to these questions, in many large companies, even though there can be a large number of people, they are grouped in multiple subdivisions. Discovering the target audience who are impacted by the project is a key to success.

How Does It Impact the Business?

Often this information may be included in some way in the contract or Charter since it feeds the Business Case for investing time and money in the project. However, it is important for you to understand the assumptions utilized to build the Business Case. These are much more specific in what the problem costs the business and why. You should try to uncover who arrived at the assumptions and/or how. This is important because it may very well be that your sponsor provided the Business Case assumptions.

How Does This Problem/Issue Impact the Sponsor's Role and Responsibilities?

Here you are getting very precise about what is at stake for your sponsor. For example, if your sponsor tells you that this project or initiative is part of a change in strategy or direction for the company, you must realize that the sponsor is probably accountable to the president of the division, at a minimum, if not the CEO.

What Other Options Did You Consider?

Receiving the answer to this question will help you understand why your project was sanctioned in the first place and why your sponsor was chosen. The answer here is important because, as issues arise in your project as they always do, you won't want to suggest a solution that was already considered and rejected by the executive team.

I remember quite clearly that I was leading a systems project, and during the course of the technical work, we discovered that we had to change the configuration significantly from where we started. The problem was that this particular option had been considered and rejected by the senior management team as too expensive when they sanctioned the project. The technical team leads and I had to make the case that the only way this project could be a success would be to utilize the rejected option. We considered this option to be the best one, so we knew we had to be prepared to provide convincing evidence that would change the minds of senior management. It also had an impact on the Business Case. We had to recognize that senior management might shut down the project.

The first step was to clearly explain the situation to the sponsor and get her to agree that this was the right answer to solving the problem. She suggested that we gather additional data that would support the recommendation because she knew where the resistance would come from and what information might sway those individuals.

Then she and I set up meetings to presell the idea to those key individuals. We were not going to the full Steering Committee with this recommendation until we knew we had the support of key decision makers.

Through following these steps, we were prepared for the Steering Committee. I was definitely grilled about the change, particularly why we had no other options to offer. My sponsor was great in that she defended the recommendations of the team knowing that she had the support of other executives in the room. Our recommendation was accepted and allowed us to successfully deliver the project.

How Frequently Does This Problem Occur?

This question should help you uncover the root cause of the issue/problem that the project was designed to fix. You need to be able to determine the area where that root cause lies. It may be:

- People
- Materials
- Equipment
- Procedures

It is helpful to remember that often problems that people see are sometimes only symptoms of the real problem and that their perspective is influenced by the symptom they view. The answer to this question will help you to understand the answers you have received to your earlier questions and provide context for the next question.

It is important to remember that projects often uncover bad business practices that are out of scope for a project. You will need to work with your sponsor to ensure you don't get dragged into a war over fixing the poor practice. The best way to address the issue and not get caught up in scope creep is to ask your sponsor to establish a working group outside the team with a charge to bring a recommendation that will address this business practice.

What Would You Like to Be Able to Do?

Asking this question will help you to unlock two keys that are important for a project to succeed:

1. Understanding what is really new about the solution this project is providing and
2. Acceptance criteria for the solution.

However, remember that often a sponsor may be someone who has not been "in the trenches" for quite a while. You might think about taking the answer and discussing it with some key, friendly managers who actually supervise the work that is done. These people are often at the director level in most large organizations. These people frequently have one foot in each world—both operational and strategic. Just remember that if these directors report to the sponsor, politics are involved as well. So as part of your discussion, you may want to paraphrase what you have heard so that there is an understanding that these are your words rather than the sponsor's words. If you receive answers that are somewhat different (I doubt you will hear something that is a complete disconnect), you can circle back to the sponsor and get further clarification on the solution. It is important that you satisfy both your sponsor and those directors.

Also, you are trying to gather information on the acceptance criteria for the solution. Be sure to get as many details as possible. If someone says the solution should save time, be sure you get a definition about how much time they are talking about. And define who's saving that time. If they mention that the process should be more streamlined, determine how they would assess whether a new process is more streamlined. In all this, you are seeking the acceptance criteria for your project.

One risk a project manager faces while determining the acceptance criteria can be that there are gross misunderstandings and inflated expectations. Too many times vendors have sold a solution to senior management and that vendor has been fast and loose with the facts. If you believe your sponsor has been a victim, you will need to discuss that as soon as you have enough evidence to reset expectations. I will provide more guidance on how to handle this situation in Chapter 13.

What Constraints, Assumptions, and Complexities Exist for Delivering the Project?

For example, you need to understand the assumptions that were used to build the Business Case. As part of your risk assessment, you will need to do some what-if scenarios should circumstances change the reality behind the assumptions. This will be particularly important if you have a project that takes a year or more to complete. You should discuss these potential risks with your sponsor to make certain that they agree with your mitigation strategy. If they don't, they will probably offer their own mitigation, which is even better because they will defend that strategy if the risk becomes an issue.

Another key element involves the complexities related to these assumptions. As an illustration, a project that I led involved the installation of upgrades on oceangoing ships. However, the upgrade could occur only when the vessels were in port and docked. Clearly one constraint was getting our team members to the port locations at the same time as the ships arrived. Any changes in the shipping schedule automatically changed our schedule.

As you can imagine, we had delays while installing the systems on the ships, and I needed my sponsor and champion to support me when changes occurred that were beyond my control.

Points to Remember

- Review the questions from this chapter, and see which ones are relevant to you and your project.
- Be sure you understand the impact to the business.
- Other options considered are important for you to know.
- Identify constraints, assumptions, and complexities from your sponsor's point of view.

4

Establishing the Relationship and Managing Up the Organization

TO BETTER UNDERSTAND how to build the relationship and manage up the organization, I want to revisit some of the basic concepts from Chapter 1. You will remember that executives spend a lot of time considering a project before making a decision. Once the decision is made, the only one on the executive team who is still concerned about its success is your sponsor. To be clear, it is not that other executives don't care; it is just that it is not on their plate to deliver, so it is "out of sight, out of mind," as the old saying goes.

The other concept from the facts of life involves the political stakes and the importance to your sponsor that there is a perception of control and stability within the project. It is within this environment that you will begin to build a relationship with your sponsor.

Building a Relationship and Trust

To understand why building a relationship with your sponsor is so important, we need to recognize that relationships are built on trust.

Webster's dictionary defines trust as a "firm belief in the reliability, truth, ability, or strength of someone or something."

While it may seem a cliché to say that relationships are built on trust, it is the absolute truth. It doesn't matter if it is a marriage, friendship, or a workplace relationship, trust is absolutely essential.

So why is trust important between a project manager and the sponsor? When a relationship is built on trust, there is a sense of authenticity, acceptance, forgiveness, and openness. Once trust is weakened or if trust is absent, people tend to hide their true feelings and information.

The building blocks of trust are:

- Credibility: "I believe what you say."
- Reliability: "I can depend on you."
- Intimacy: "I feel comfortable discussing this with you, and I know you care about me and the business."
- Personal integrity: "I have confidence that you are honest and have moral principles."

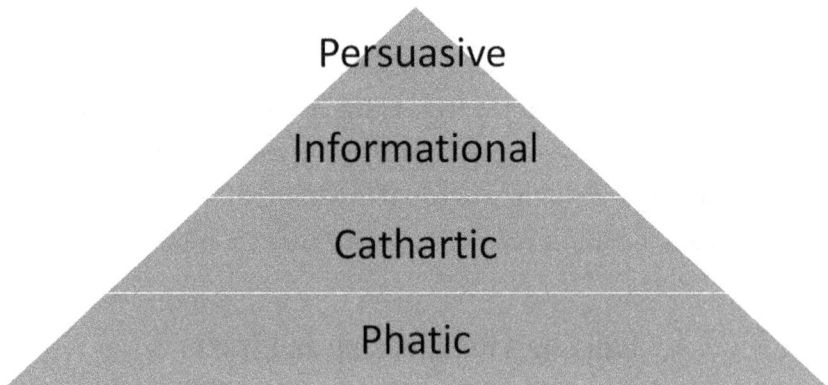

Persuasive

Informational

Cathartic

Phatic

Figure 4.1: The Hierarchy of Communications

Building trust and a relationship can also depend on how you communicate to your sponsor. When we think about communications, we usually think about sending and receiving information. However, that is only one form of communication. In fact, there is a hierarchy for communications (see Figure 4.1):

- *Phatic* communications are the lowest-level but the real foundation of developing a relationship. Phatic communications are defined as communication used for social purposes and establishing a relationship rather than communicating information.
- *Cathartic* communications are used to provide relief or tension through open expression of strong emotions. The point here is that at times a sponsor may appear upset with you or the project, but other issues might be going on, so don't jump to conclusions.
- *Informational* communications are well understood as passing data or content back and forth.
- *Persuasive* communications are used to change someone's mind or opinion. A project manager would be smart to hold back on using this form of communication until he has firmly established his relationship with the sponsor.

Achieving Credibility

For you as a project manager to achieve credibility with a sponsor, you must consistently demonstrate your expertise not only by providing information but through the types of questions you ask and assertions you make.

Achieving Reliability

You will achieve a perception of reliability for demonstrating a commitment to accuracy and completeness in your work. That does not mean giving a sponsor so much detail that they can't keep up but rather tailoring the information to the type of details that your sponsor requires. Finally, reliability is a demonstrated commitment to resolving problems quickly and in a manner that addresses stakeholder concerns.

Attaining Intimacy

A project manager will develop a trusting relationship with a sponsor by consistently demonstrating a commitment to helping the sponsor achieve the business goals of the project. That commitment will allow a project manager and a sponsor to engage in joint problem solving through a willingness to speak openly and candidly with each other.

Demonstrating Integrity

One of the most important traits that will build trust is demonstrating integrity. In the first chapter, I discussed the sometimes difficult political environment that your sponsor may find himself in with regard to your project. The sponsor really needs to feel that you "have his back." That means that you have to keep the sponsor informed and that he is never surprised when confronted or questioned about the project.

Figuring Out How to Stay in Touch

One of the biggest hurdles for a project manager is staying in touch with a senior manager. If your senior management is anything like the ones I have had the pleasure of working with, just getting on their calendar for a meeting can be a real challenge. While it is counterintuitive for us, the reality is that senior managers often have less control over their schedules than you do! If you ever got the chance to really look at their calendars, you would see that most of them spend their day moving from one meeting to the next. That explains why they are late to most meetings: Once one meeting runs over the agenda time, it has a domino effect on the rest of their day. Too often, your meeting to discuss project-related matters is seen as one place they can cancel to catch up with other meetings. The reason goes back to the realities explained in Chapter 1: Your project is part of the business that is future oriented, and the work that is operational will always take precedent over your project. So how to overcome that problem?

One way that I have used that has been very successful is to schedule breakfast with my sponsor. Most senior executives that I have worked with are quite used to coming to the office early. At times an early start is the period of time when they can actually get some work done before all the interruptions begin. So see if you can get your sponsor to meet you for breakfast on a regular basis. If he is traveling at the time you have a regularly scheduled meeting, work with him or his assistant to reschedule it based on wherever he is at the time. However, try to keep in mind his time zone and location, and do your best to schedule it either before or after the normal working hours in that location even if it means you are talking to him very late at night or very early in the morning. Believe me when I tell you that any inconvenience you experience will be made up for many times over.

Determining Whether a Champion Can Help

There may be times when a champion can help you in managing up the chain. I would describe a champion as a person who has a high level of interest in the project and who has a positive attitude toward the project. Often a champion can have a powerful influence on other managers because she is perceived as very good at her job and understands very well "how things work around here." She can be a great sounding board for you as you try to navigate the politics and conflicting stakeholder priorities because she knows the business so well. If the champion reports to the sponsor, all the better! In that case, she may have more access to the sponsor because of that reporting relationship. The champion might be a conduit for you to the sponsor and also provide you with insights into how the sponsor thinks about certain issues or decisions. Either way, make a concerted effort to develop a relationship with a champion if you don't have one already.

Points to Remember

- Understand how to build a relationship and establish trust.
- Achieve credibility.
- Realize reliability.
- Attain intimacy.
- Demonstrate integrity.
- Figure out how you will stay in touch.
- Determine whether a champion can help you.

5

Working with the Executive Sponsor to Understand the Project

Collaborating on the Charter

The first way to engage your sponsor is to begin by drafting the Charter for the project. The Project Management Institute (PMI) defines the *Charter* as a formal document that approves the start of the project. I do not actually share that view. I believe the Charter serves as a great communication tool between the project manager and the sponsor. Review the Business Case, the proposal (if one was developed), and the contract if there is one. From all these documents, write a draft Charter including:

- Background on the project, including the business problem the project should resolve.
- Business benefits expected to be delivered.
- Scope of the project.
- Deliverables to be produced.
- Timeline and budget.

Working with the Sponsor on Scope

However, there are key items where collaboration with your sponsor can be really valuable. First, and most importantly, determine what is:

- In scope
- Out of scope

In my experience over the years, there is usually general agreement on what is in scope. However, where things get dicey for the project manager is in determining what is out of scope. For example, many of my projects are the delivery of new systems for use in the business. Often the contract, or the Statement of Work, will include training. That is fine as far as it goes. However, I usually interpret that as the typical out-of-the-box training included with any implementation. However, many times when I highlight that customized training is out of scope, I get a pushback from the sponsor. He was expecting the training to be tied to exactly the way we installed and calibrated the system for users. Now reflect for a moment on the implications of that.

As you can imagine, training usually comes near the end of the project as we are preparing to go live. What if the last phase of the project is when I found out that customized training was expected? It would be a disaster. If I had included customized training as out of scope in the Charter, there are two possible outcomes that are much better.

1. My sponsor corrects my expectation right at the beginning, and I adjust my scope accordingly and include the customized training in my plan.
2. The sponsor does not correct me, and a key stakeholder expresses disappointment in the training offered because it was too general. At that point I can correctly assert that the

sponsor agreed that customized training was out of scope. The focus of the issue has changed. In that scenario, the key stakeholder has an issue with the sponsor, not with me as the project manager!

Measures of Success

Another key element is getting the measures of success according to my sponsor. For example, recall that in one of my early projects, the requirement was to all users to create reports faster. We worked hard and delivered what we thought was a successful project. The problem was that I had failed to ask my sponsor how he defined "faster." We had cut the time required to produce the reports by 20%. However, my sponsor had expected that we would cut the time in half! My lesson learned was always to make sure I understood how "success" was being measured from the beginning. It is the same concept we all used when we were in college; we wanted to know from the beginning, "How do I get an A in this class?"

Clarifying the Assumptions

In the Charter, I also want to include any assumptions and/or constraints that I perceive as part of the project. For example, in some of the systems projects, the installation of the system is on large, ocean-going ships. A constraint we have on the project is that the vessels must be in port in order to install the system. The assumption is that we have an accurate schedule of when various ships will be in port so that we can build the project schedule and deploy our project resources accordingly. By working with our sponsor on the Charter, which includes these constraints and assumptions, if a ship is not in port as scheduled, the impact on the project schedule is obvious, and the sponsor is far more likely to be sympathetic and protective since that was discussed right up front.

In most projects, the deliverables created will usually produce changes in the way people work. A key role for senior management is to help you explain to affected stakeholders when they ask, "Why are we doing this project anyway?"

Working on the Case for Change

In a standard format, some general questions require answers if you are to build a robust communication plan. Those questions are:

- From a business perspective, why are we doing this project?
- Why are we doing it now?
- What are the benefits of successfully completing this project?
- What are the consequences of not completing this project successfully?

Feel free to edit these questions as is appropriate for your project and your situation. These are all common questions that the vast majority of people impacted by a project are asking themselves and others each time a new initiative is proposed by management.

In creating a Case for Change, you are trying to shape a perception that builds awareness, knowledge and appreciation for the solutions you are delivering as part of the project (see Figure 5.1).

In the beginning, I always create a draft document, and I would recommend you do the same, so that your sponsor can correct and/or apply it. In most cases, it is far better to come in with a draft document that the sponsor can react to. Some project managers I have talked to have tried to start with a blank sheet of paper, and the exercise ended in a real disaster. Sponsors do not want to spend the time required to start from scratch. Even when you start with a well drafted document,

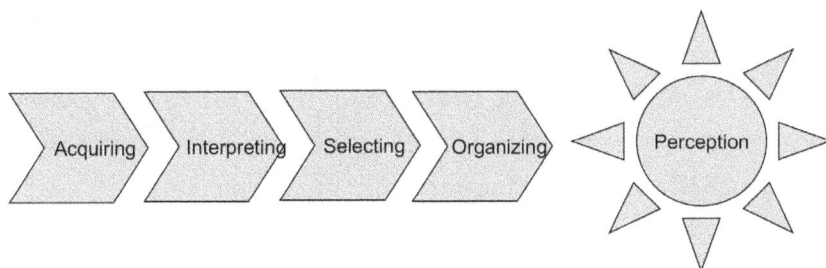

Figure 5.1: Classic Process of Perception

you will still learn significant and valuable information just trying to edit it with the sponsor!

Of course, the purpose for the Case for Change is not to document all the gory details like cost/benefit analysis, return on investment, net present value, and so on. However, if you have a well drafted Business Case, you can usually glean many of the answers to the questions posed earlier—at least enough to provide the draft for the sponsor. As project manager, you need to engage your sponsor and then other key stakeholders to determine their answers to these questions. Please realize that some people may not be able to answer them in everyday language. They may tend to give you language that is typical of the standard Business Case, so you will have to interpret and paraphrase to test your understanding. Determining whether key leaders have significantly different answers from your sponsor's is useful to both of you. The sponsor will need to confer with her colleagues to make sure of alignment and expectations.

Get Inside the Head of the Sponsor

There is another key purpose in working with the sponsor to address these questions: The answers you receive help you "get inside the head" of the sponsor or other key executives. Remember in Chapter 1 when I addressed the environment where projects are sanctioned? I mentioned that the leadership team has considered many options and decided on your project for execution. Working with your sponsor to answer these questions should give you some context for the answers. You were not privy to the discussions, and your sponsor might fail to give you that background unless prompted. Hopefully, working with you on the Case for Change will jog her memory and help you tremendously.

Deliverable/Activity	Requirement
Charter	Collaborate as a communication tool
Scope	Confirm scope, especially out-of-scope activities
Measures of Success	Define exactly how the project will be seen as a success
Identify Assumptions	Business case but might also include constraints
Case for Change	Answer the questions about "why" related to the project
Presenting Information	Strategy and purpose for each communication

Figure 5.2: Working with the Project Sponsor

Presenting Information to the Sponsor

As you can see, I am suggesting an entire series of steps to establish your relationship with the sponsor in Figure 5.2. Each step will help you understand how the sponsor views the project and what is really important to them. That allows you to choose which strategy to use later on when you must present information to the sponsor.

In presenting material on the project to the sponsor, I have used a variety of strategies for organizing the information. I will first take you through the strategies, and then I will explain how I choose the one that might be appropriate.

- **Big Picture/Small Picture:** I have found that this strategy is very persuasive to senior management because it explains how the project is progressing against the business goals that the project is trying to achieve. I work very hard to tie the data and information directly to those goals. I have found that if you cannot make a clear correlation to one of the goals, then do not use that information. I am not saying it might not be useful. You may have it as backup in case the data could be used to answer a question.

- **Problem/Solution:** When I am reporting on problems or issues related to the project, this strategy can be very effective. In this approach, I may cycle back and forth between problems that the project is encountering and the solutions that the project team is working on. To be most effective, I attempt to think about exactly the questions that the sponsor would want answered and make sure to have the information to answer them and to illustrate how the information supports the recommended solution. Another variation of this strategy is the question/answer technique. You take the questions you believe the sponsor will have regarding your project and work your way through the questions and answers. Either way, the goal is to assure your sponsor that you have the problems clearly identified and that you are working on solutions. Remember, from a political perspective, appearing to have the project under control is very important!

- **Most Critical to Least Critical:** I have found this approach is very useful if I find that my time with the sponsor always seems to be shorter than originally scheduled. Under those circumstances, I always start with the most critical information for the sponsor and work my way through to the material that could be left out without compromising the sponsor's understanding of the progress and status of the project. That way, if I am cut short of time, I can be confident that I have covered all of the most important items.

- **Contrast/Compare:** This strategy is quite useful if a recent project had problems and my sponsor is concerned about ending up in the same situation, remembering the political costs from the previous project. In this approach, I want to update the sponsor and explain how this project is different (contrast) and how this project is being handled more effectively. Then I point out how the current project may look somewhat the same as the earlier project (compare) but that the project team is handling the issues much better. At times, I have reversed the order and covered the "compare" section first and then followed with the "contrast" information.

So now let's look at how I choose which strategy I might employ.

The first consideration is to understand the purpose of my update.

What do you want your sponsor to:

- Know
- Do
- Feel

When presenting information to your sponsor, you should be able to complete this sentence:

"The purpose of providing this information is …"

I decide what the purpose is and work from there. I have always believed that people who think that the information will speak for itself are completely wrong. Please recognize that using the strategies I have just described is certainly providing information to the sponsor. However, a good friend of mine called the same old schedule/cost/issues briefing as the weather report. In labeling it that way, he meant that there is information but very little that would engage the sponsor. No doubt the information in a weather report might be useful, but do not get into that rut. I want my sponsor to understand the information the way I do.

So after I decide the purpose, I decide which strategy will help me achieve my purpose. In that respect, I often change the strategy from time to time. In fact, I may lay out a couple of options and determine which one works best. For example, if my project needs a decision that requires input from the sponsor, I will try out the problem/solution strategy and then the question/answer strategy to decide which approach will be more effective in eliciting the sponsor's help.

If my purpose requires the sponsor to engage with or get consensus from other executive stakeholders, then I might frame the information using big picture/little picture because it will probably be far more helpful. The rationale is to discuss business outcomes and not technical details, which may or may not be of interest to the other stakeholders.

The second consideration in presenting information to my sponsor is based on the person and how she utilizes information. At the highest level, I have found there are two key considerations for sponsors:

1. **What is their approach to information?** I have found that some people are fact oriented and therefore I must use data. However, others will be concept oriented. For those people, I use ideas. I recognize that I may be perceived as stereotyping people, but here are some examples related to sponsors I have worked with.

   a. Many of my projects have been for engineers or IT people. For those sponsors, I focus heavily on the data because they will challenge me if I do not produce it.

   b. Other projects have been for people in human resources or training/talent management. For those sponsors, I must be more idea oriented.

2. **What is their approach to outcomes?** Some sponsors are results oriented and therefore I focus on the "what" so that they can process the information. Others are more people oriented, and so I must focus on how things will happen.

      a. For sponsors who are results oriented, I have to focus on the specific steps to achieve the results and what the risks are to the outcome.

      b. As for other sponsors who focus on people, I will never forget one of my sponsors and the first question he always asked me: "Who will be mad at me if we do this?" Every time! That may be an extreme example, but these people are genuinely concerned about how people will react to information.

So as you prepare to work with your sponsor, remember:

- Collaborate on the Charter to find alignment.
- Work to understand the scope of the project, particularly what is out of scope.
- Recognize the measures of success so you know how you will be judged.
- Get inside the head of the sponsor so you understand how to work with her.
- Use a strategy for presenting information to your sponsor that matches your purpose and how she utilizes that information.

Points to Remember

- Collaborate with the sponsor on the Charter as a communication document.
- Work with the sponsor to define the scope.
- Identify measures of success before the project starts.
- Clarify all assumptions at the beginning.
- Collaborate with the sponsor on the Case for Change.
- Understand how your sponsor thinks.
- Plan carefully when presenting information to the sponsor.

6

Reviewing the Stakeholder Analysis with Your Sponsor

IT IS COMMON practice for project managers to complete a stakeholder analysis as part of the planning for a project. However, in this chapter, I am suggesting that you review the analysis with only those executives who are stakeholders, not everyone involved. There are a variety of ways to complete a stakeholder analysis, but executives will have a different way of viewing executive stakeholders than a project manager would. Here are some ideas that should help you have a conversation and work with your sponsor to plan the engagement with other key executive stakeholders.

As suggested in the previous chapter, my experience is that you should draft your own answers to these questions and then work with your sponsor to revise them into a more complete and appropriate document.

Who Are the Key Stakeholders Who Care about the Project, and Who Will Be Affected by the Deliverables?

All project managers know that the classic definition of a stakeholder is a person or group who may be affected by the outcomes of the project. As stated earlier, it is a good bet that your sponsor was chosen because his division has the most to gain from the successful outcome of the project—and therefore may have a lot to lose! For your sponsor, the stakeholders he will be most concerned with are those whose divisions or departments are impacted by the deliverables your project is producing. If you doubt that, please refer back to Chapter 1 on the facts of life for executives.

Classifying Stakeholders

The latest thinking about stakeholders is to analyze the power they can have over the project and/or decisions affecting the project. The classification of that power generally breaks down into four groups:

1. The authority they have in the organization and how that authority can allow them to impose their ideas on the project
2. The influence (particularly technical expertise) they have in the planning or execution of the project or even veto power regarding certain decisions
3. Involvement in the project, which could include people seconded to the project or participation in the Steering Committee (I'll talk about this later) as examples
4. The level of concern or interest in the outcomes of the project

The output of your identification and classification will become input into your communication and engagement plan.

On large projects, you can also identify different stakeholder types such as:

- Champion: Powerful with a high level of interest and a positive attitude. Pay attention to the champion at all times.
- Friend: Low power but high interest in the project with a positive attitude. Use friends as a sounding board.
- Sleeping giant: Powerful, who support the project but display low levels of interest or enthusiasm. You need to raise the giant's level of interest.
- Acquaintance: Low power and low interest, who just need to be informed from time to time
- Time bomb: Powerful with a high level of interest but a negative attitude. Must be actively engaged and diffused to prevent a major disruption of the project.

Conduct an Impact Analysis

Before working with the sponsor, I like to get my team leads, business analysts, and other appropriate subject matter experts (SMEs) and do a preliminary impact analysis.

The impact analysis starts with various processes and/or workflows that will be directly impacted by the changes brought on by the project. I will return to this analysis later in the project as we begin to execute the work because things may change or our assessment of the impact may change.

After looking at the workflow or process, I would recommend you conduct a preliminary estimate on the magnitude of the change. In some of my projects, the impact has been minimal, and others have been quite dramatic. For example, in some of my systems projects, for some user stakeholders, the change might be simply in the location of navigation buttons they use to move around within the application. For other user stakeholders, the changes go way beyond simple navigation. The changes may include the way they use the system—an entirely new way of accessing and handling the information that they use to complete their work.

This type of assessment will be important to have available as you discuss various stakeholders with your sponsor. All of these people eventually report up to one of the sponsor's peers. This should help your conversation about some of the answers to the stakeholder analysis. In my experience, this evaluation can be a real benefit. At times, I and my team did not realize there were some additional ramifications related to these stakeholders that were not visible to us but were to the sponsor. I have received excellent input from my sponsor on how to deal with certain people. I have also been able to identify risks that would not have been on my risk register if I had not had the conversation.

Within that context, identify the individuals who will care about the work you are doing. Remember to think at the higher level of a division or department that each executive oversees and how that group is impacted. These people may be vice presidents or directors as well as managers. With your sponsor, you want to work to answer these two specific questions:

1. What is this executive's responsibility, and how will her span of control be impacted by your project?
2. Should this executive have some responsibility to the project itself?

What Is This Executive's Responsibility, and How Will Her Span of Control Be Impacted by Your Project?

If we return to the earlier discussion about politics and leadership, there is only a small chance that another executive will have as much interest as your executive sponsor. However, executives are quite sensitive to complaints that come to their attention as the project progresses. I always talk to my sponsor about what various stakeholders know about the project. I would put my project and my reputation at risk if I assume various stakeholders know more about the project than they really do.

One of the key questions to have answered from your sponsor relates to the governance of the project. For example, will this stakeholder be part of the Steering Committee or governance board of the project? If they are part of the governance structure, then it is important for you to understand why they are on the Steering Committee so that you can determine what their role will be. If they are not part of the governance structure, and you think it would seem natural for them to be on a Steering Committee, it is very important to find out why they were not offered a seat at the table. In my experience when that has happened, what I learned was that they are sponsoring another project and just don't have the time to give to your project. That is a reasonable business decision, but I still want to discuss with my sponsor our approach to keeping such executives informed about my project. My biggest fear would be that the only information they have about my project is through the rumor mill. Another big risk is that their perception of the project is only through complaints brought to them by their people.

It is important to understand that executives will almost always support the people who report to them. I heard one project manager express it this way: "They will never blame their people. That is like telling someone that their baby is ugly." You just cannot win in that scenario.

What Is This Stakeholder's Level of Support or Interest?

I also ask my sponsor to judge the level of support and/or interest of each stakeholder. This is another key element where the impact analysis can be of assistance.

In a project we did that involved implementing a customer relationship management (CRM) system, I had the type of situation I am warning you about.

To simplify for the sake of illustration, the CRM is a very robust database that tracks all of the information on a customer. It tracks from the front end of the value chain, from sales to order fulfillment, and on to invoicing. Some examples of customer data are:

- Key personnel and locations.
- Contracts in place with divisions and locations.
- Past buying patterns and potential discounts.
- Credit limits.
- Orders in process of fulfillment.
- Outstanding invoices.

I think it is apparent that just about every department in the company would be impacted by the CRM. However, each of them had a very different perspective on what was important. For example, the:

- The vice president of sales was interested in how she could assist her team in driving more sales.
- The general manager of operations was most concerned about the accuracy of the orders as a way to drive his

production schedule for improved efficiency and cost reduction.

■ The chief financial officer was concerned that the correct customer contracts and credit terms were included so that the company could be paid in a timely fashion to improve profit margins.

■ The vice president of customer service was most concerned that the CRM would improve customer satisfaction in annual surveys.

My sponsor in this project was the president of the company. I certainly had an advantage in that all of these people reported to my sponsor, but it also meant additional pressure for me to prevent complaints from reaching my sponsor before I could alert him. He helped me understand how to gauge each of these people as stakeholders. I asked for help in answering three questions:

1. What might they dislike about the project and why?
2. What is the best way to receive feedback from this stakeholder?
3. How can we best manage their expectations?

Here are a couple of examples. My sponsor answered the first question for the vice president of sales this way. She was very concerned that the CRM would become a bureaucratic nightmare for her team. From her perspective, she wanted the sales team out in front of customers or prospects. She was very concerned they would spend too much time in front of their laptops.

In answering question 2 for the general manager of operations, my sponsor warned me that he usually ignored e-mails, and so sending updates using that medium would be a waste of time. The suggestion was to arrange for a regular one-on-one meeting both to provide information but also to receive feedback on the project.

For question 3, the CFO was a data person, which was no surprise to me and probably is not to you either. The best way to manage his expectations was to quantify various information related to the project.

For all of the key stakeholders and my sponsor as well, the most successful way was to use pictures in graphs or charts.

In reviewing stakeholder analysis with your sponsor, be sure to:

- Conduct an impact analysis prior to the review.
- Determine what each executive's responsibilities may be in relation to the project.
- Identify each stakeholder's level of commitment and support for your project.

Points to Remember

- Classify stakeholders in collaboration with your sponsor.
- Conduct an impact analysis to determine how each stakeholder group is affected.
- Develop a role for the sponsor to play a part in the stakeholder engagement plan.
- Be sure you understand each stakeholder's level of commitment to your project.

7

Listening Styles and How Using Them Effectively Helps You to Engage an Executive

IN UNDERSTANDING THE listening styles of individuals, including your sponsor, we have to first go back to the basics of communication itself.

Review:
- Audience/Target
- Sensitivities/Barriers
- Purpose
- Details
- Formal versus informal
- Jargon and acronyms

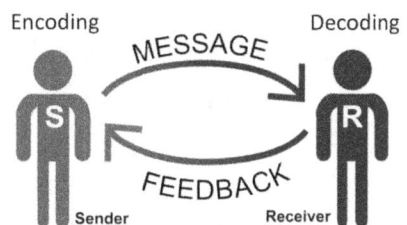

Encoding   MESSAGE   Decoding

S   R

FEEDBACK

Sender   Receiver

Figure 7.1: Common Elements for All Communications

As Figure 7.1 shows, the most common process for communication to occur involves encoding and decoding. A speaker encodes an idea or information using the language that is common to both people. This communication can be in oral or written form. The listener then decodes the message for understanding. If the listener is not certain about the meaning, then he gives the speaker feedback, and the back-and-forth continues. On the face of it, that may sound simple, but it is really quite complex once you begin to dig deeper.

Basics for Communication

For example, the language used for business around the world is English. That is good news for me because I do not speak any other language well enough to conduct business in it. And I admire people who speak more than one language. Now let me illustrate how even that can be complicated.

I was working on the project plan for a major project in Romania. The project team members were people from three countries: Romania, Russia, and Serbia. Because of that, the only language they had in common was English. But consider for a moment that for all of them, including my sponsor, English was a second language. Please keep in mind that the project was highly technical in nature. I had to be very aware during the discussions to ensure that everyone understood the tasks and activities the same way. My method for doing that was to continually seek feedback to check for common understanding.

During projects I have led with team members from the United Kingdom, there was no guarantee of common understanding even though the Americans and British share English as their first language.

Furthermore, people may "check out" during long meetings. The U.S. Navy Air Warfare Center Training Systems Division did a study to find out how well people listen. They discovered that most people focus for about 18 minutes attentively, and then their focus diminishes. The other interesting fact the Navy learned was that people remembered about only 25% of what they heard if they did not take notes or have some form of recording the discussion.

Understanding that finding reminds me that, when I am in discussions with my sponsor, I have to be very aware of the potential for him to lose focus. Several of my colleagues believe that their executives all suffer from some form of attention deficit disorder (ADD), but I really believe that what they are experiencing is this built-in focus issue. So how do we handle that?

Listening Styles

First of all, Kittie Watson, PhD, and Larry Barker, PhD, have done some great work in helping people understand the listening styles that people employ. The styles they identify are:

- People-oriented: They are concerned with how people will react.
- Action-oriented: They want someone to get to the point quickly.
- Content-oriented: They value technical information and data.
- Time-oriented: They are very conscious of time, particularly wasting time.[1]

Each of these listening styles has both strengths and weaknesses. Let's look at each of them in more detail.

PEOPLE-ORIENTED LISTENERS

Strengths	Weaknesses
• Concerned about others • Nonjudgmental • Provide clear feedback both verbally and nonverbally • Notice others moods quickly • Interested in building relationships	• May get overly involved with others' feelings • Avoid seeing faults in people • Internalize emotional state of others • Can be overly expressive • May not discriminate enough in building relationships

ACTION-ORIENTED LISTENERS

Strengths	Weaknesses
• Get to the point quickly • Give clear feedback on expectations • Concentrate on the task at hand • Help others focus and encourage others to be organized • Identify inconsistencies in messages	• Tend to be impatient • Jump ahead and finish sentences of others • Get distracted by disorganized speakers • Ask blunt questions • May appear overly critical • May minimize relationships

CONTENT-ORIENTED LISTENERS

Strengths	Weaknesses
• Value technical information • Test for clarity and understanding • Encourage others to provide support for their ideas • Welcome complex and challenging information • Look at all sides of the issue	• May be overly detail oriented • May intimidate others by asking pointed questions • Minimize nontechnical information • Discount information from nonexperts • Take a long time to make a decision

TIME-ORIENTED LISTENERS

Strengths	Weaknesses
• Manage and save time • Set time guidelines for meetings and conversations • Let others know of time requirements • Discourage "wordy" speakers • Give cues when time is being wasted	• Tend to be impatient regarding time • Interrupt others • Let time affect their ability to concentrate • Rush speakers by looking at watch or clock • Limit creativity by imposing time limits

Does Everyone Use Only One Style?

The reality is that most people have a preferred style. Circumstances may cause any individual to adopt a different style for a time. For example, I had a sponsor who was very much a time-oriented listener. However, I saw him suppress that tendency when we were having a discussion with the person he reported to in the company.

Likewise, a normally content-oriented listener might seem to adopt a time-oriented approach if time pressures are related to a discussion.

How Do I Apply This Information?

You may be thinking about how to apply this information, and the answer to that question is very important. Obviously, the first application is to assess whom you are speaking to and work to match your verbal style to her listening style.

Purpose of the Communication

When most people think about speaking and listening in a business context, they think only of one purpose for the communication: the

- Persuasive
  - Influence
  - Motivate to act
- Informative
  - Share data and/or ideas
- Cathartic
  - Release emotions
- Phatic
  - Establish relationships

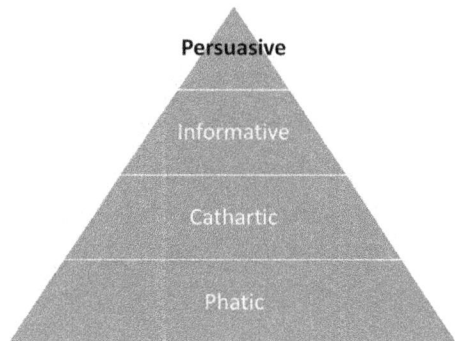

Figure 7.2: Purposes of Communication

exchange of information. However, there are actually three other purposes for speaking, and it is important to recognize them too (see Figure 7.2):

1. *Phatic* communication focuses on building relationships and often involves what most people call small talk. "How was your weekend? . . . How is the family?" It is the way we understand common interests and connections.

2. *Cathartic* communication focuses on the release of emotions. The root of the word comes from Greek and means "venting." It is the communication where emotions, such as frustration or disappointment, are released. Most of the time, people are not looking for a conversation; they are just trying to get something off their chest.

3. Finally, *persuasive* communication focuses on influencing or motivating someone to act. This is the highest level of communication and the most difficult. However, when we are working with our sponsor on issues or topics related to the project, we are usually attempting to persuade and motivate him to act on our behalf. If that is true, then how do you persuade him?

Target

The first consideration is recognizing the listening style of the sponsor and other key stakeholders. Face it, you typically are not going to persuade someone to act by sending an e-mail or writing a report. You will need to handle that face-to-face if you mean to succeed. First of all, analyze the listening style of the person you are talking to so that you can better influence her regarding the project. You may follow up with something in writing with other details if they are important.

Potential Barriers

Sensitivities and barriers are also important to consider in working with your sponsor. One that I have often faced is simply finding time in my sponsor's busy schedule. Often I need to talk to him about various issues or progress but he is traveling. Many of my sponsors have been part of global companies, so travel may involve time zone differences that require me to be considerate in how I schedule communication. In some of my projects, my sponsor has been literally halfway around the world on business. There is no convenient time in reality. In those situations, I try to think about the time zone they are in and schedule something that will work better for them than for me. Along the same line, on some projects, my sponsor has been in the Middle East where there is also a different work week. Working with your sponsor in advance can help you manage those situations.

Details

Part of working with your sponsor will be striking the correct balance related to details. I have worked with sponsors who are very interested in the details—more than I would have guessed at the beginning. Others have been more inclined to simply want the high-level information and want details only when there are issues or problems. One technique that I have used in the past has been to ask at the beginning of the project exactly how detailed they want me to get in communicating with them. This also relates to the type of listener they are. For example, as already mentioned, one sponsor would always ask me the same question related to decisions: "Who will be mad at me if we do this?" As you can probably guess, this was a people-oriented listener, and I quickly realized that should be part of any conversation related to a decision or issue.

Jargon and Acronyms

We all know that business is full of jargon and acronyms. So is project management. Be very sensitive to using either jargon or acronyms when talking with your sponsor. As an example, in one automation project I led, without really thinking about it, I started using some jargon that was very common in the IT and data world. I did not find out until a little later that my sponsor did not know what I was referring to with that language. I found out after we had built a good relationship that she was a little embarrassed to tell me she did not know what I meant. Naturally, I felt badly and vowed to watch my use of jargon and acronyms in the future, not just with her but in all future projects. I have also found that I was using project management jargon that was not understood by some of my key stakeholders. For example, I would make a remark about the WBS (work breakdown statement). Now all of you reading this book probably know exactly what that means, but these key stakeholders did not.

So as you plan your discussions with the sponsor or other key stakeholders, work very hard to avoid that pitfall. I would also encourage you to discuss that with your sponsors as you are building your relationship. Let them know that you might, unwittingly, start using jargon that they are unfamiliar with and that they should ask for clarification if it ever happens.

Formal versus Informal

As you are working with your sponsor and learning their listening style, it is also helpful to learn how formal they like their discussions to be. I have had sponsors who preferred to sit in the cafeteria and discuss the project over coffee. I have had others who wanted any discussions related to the project to be in their office with the doors closed. Of course, certain situations require a closed-door meeting, but some of my sponsors just preferred that venue regardless of the topic.

If you have a sponsor who is less formal, you must still be vigilant that people do not eavesdrop on your conversation if you are in, say, the break room.

Points to Remember

- Remember the basics for any communication.
- Assess the listening style of your sponsor and key stakeholders.
- Apply both of these points in communicating about your project.
- Consider how formal your communication needs to be.

8

Your Attitude and Its Role in Engaging an Executive

IN MANAGING YOUR sponsor and other executives, your attitude may be the most important factor in the success of your project. After all, you are the expert in projects, not the sponsor. They are counting on you to deliver the project that is very important to them. Never underestimate the value you bring to a successful project. Attitude is defined by *Merriam-Webster's* as "the way you think or feel about something that affects a person's behavior."

> Ability is what you're capable of doing.
>
> Motivation determines what you do.
>
> Attitude determines how well you do it.
>
> *Lou Holtz, College Football Hall of Fame*
> *Coach and Motivational Speaker*

Clearly I am not talking about giving orders but rather about helping sponsors recognize how important they are to the project as well as to the company. Too often, project managers get caught up in the chain of command and do not recognize that one of the key roles they have is to provide guidance to their sponsor and other executives.

In working with my sponsor, I work hard to provide valuable insights and information related to the project, particularly the stakeholders. The attitude that I convey to them continually is that I will cover their back as the project progresses. I even establish a sort of "secret code" with them related to e-mails, as one example.

Alerting the Sponsor

Most of the time, my sponsor gets literally hundreds of e-mails every day—and will usually read those e-mails on a smart phone. The obvious conclusion is that most of those messages will be read in either a cursory way or ignored altogether. When I feel they need to know something right away, I will tell them that I will inform them in two steps.

1. I will write a relatively detailed e-mail with the relevant information and action they need to take or know about because a key stakeholder might be approaching them about it.
2. I send them a text message to their mobile phone with a brief message that they should read the e-mail from me as soon as possible.

Most of the time, I cannot give them song and verse for everything, but they are not surprised if approached about the information or issue. Most of the time, we have a meeting or phone call as soon as it is practical so that I can provide even more details to enhance their understanding.

If you are like me, you recognize that your sponsor probably has technical people who report to her and whose opinion and insights she regards as valuable. For example, if the sponsor is the vice president of human resources, she probably has not been involved in benefits management in quite a while. However, she has a manager whom she trusts to know the answers if asked. I want to be that same type of advisor as it relates to the project.

Use the Sponsor to Gain Credibility

As an example, in one of my projects, my sponsor was a vice president, and he had a key role in providing credibility to the key stakeholders—in short, they respected him very much. As part of keeping our stakeholders informed, the project team had scheduled a town hall–type meeting in the afternoon after the financial markets had closed. I really needed the vice president to be there to show support and answer questions that only he could answer if they came up. However, he was hoping to leave around lunchtime that day to fly to a meeting with an important customer. It is obvious I had to ask him to consider changing his flight so he would be available for the meeting. I reminded him that we had discussed the town hall before as part of the communication plan and why we had decided it would be important for him to attend. Like many busy executives, he had forgotten the timing of the meeting when he asked travel services to schedule his flight. In the end he decided to attend because he:

- Understood the importance of his role in that meeting.
- Valued my input on why one of his surrogates could not serve that same role.

It meant a lot of inconvenience for him, not to mention a very long day, but he did it. After the meeting, he commented that he had made the right choice because one of the questions he had to field that day could not have been handled by anyone else. I complemented him for his decision and told him I appreciated the sacrifice he was making for the sake of the project. Please trust me when I tell you that at the executive level, people do not receive compliments often unless they are the self-serving type. For me, it confirmed that I was regarded as a trusted advisor by this VP.

Another reason you will need a positive attitude has to do with the resistance to change that your project will encounter. Make no mistake that key stakeholders will push back because you are changing the way they complete their work as a result of completing the project deliverables. You will need your sponsor's help to address that resistance.

Getting Help with People Who Are Blockers

One of the most difficult situations I have ever faced concerned a manager who absolutely refused to cooperate with the project team. He was the operations manager at a plant where the team was implementing a new automation system. To successfully implement the system, we absolutely had to involve some of the operators at the plant. We needed them to help us by providing various settings and tolerances so that we could calibrate the system correctly under the conditions at that location. The manager refused to allow his people to have any time with us to complete the tasks. The irony was that his rationale was his operators' lack of time, while the Business Case for implementing the automation system was to free up operators' time from tasks that could be handled by the automation system! I had at least three meetings with the manager in an attempt to break the stalemate. Finally, I felt that I had no choice but to escalate the problem to my sponsor. My sponsor had no line authority over this operations manager. I also knew very well that the manager and my sponsor, who was part of a technical directorate, did not care for each other personally or professionally. However, without some sort of intervention, the only option I could envision would be to abandon the project at that particular location. As you can imagine, I was mortified that it had come to this end.

Fortunately, I had established the escalation process early in the project. (I will cover this in more detail in Chapter 16.) When I asked for the meeting, I provided my sponsor with an agenda on the topics and some advanced documentation to read in advance.

My attitude was stated right at the beginning of the meeting—I needed my sponsor's advice on how to proceed under the circumstances. I referenced the advanced materials and brought some backup information just in case. We discussed our options and what it might take to solve the problem. In the end, my sponsor decided that he would have to approach the general manager who supervised the region where the plant was located and who was also the person in charge of the operations manager.

While I waited for the meeting between the sponsor and general manager to happen, I simply had to put the project on hold at that location. Ultimately, the general manager "persuaded" the operation manager to allow his people to work with us.

When we scheduled the time for the team to descend on the plant, I reminded the team members that our attitude would be positive and professional. It was not our usual practice, but I decided that I needed to accompany the technical people in order to be the target of any negative behavior that might occur. I persuaded my sponsor that he should absorb the charges for my time or expenses in this situation. He agreed.

We finished the work and moved on to other locations. Needless to say, I don't receive any Christmas cards from the operations manager, but he did receive the benefits of a job well-done. I was proud that our team had kept the proper attitude. Our sponsor also appreciated that our attitude had not aggravated an already difficult relationship between the two of them.

Danger Signs

There are some danger signs that mean your positive attitude and approach might be slipping and that you will need to address the issue sooner rather than later. Believe me when I tell you that when these danger signs begin, they seldom correct themselves if your attitude is to ignore them. Here are those signs:

1. If your sponsor is not willing to tackle the tough situations, you will be in for difficult times. This directly relates to the situation I just described.
2. The executive says all the right words but does not act on them. Words without the corresponding deeds will put the project in serious risk, as we all know.
3. The sponsor begins to delegate some of her critical leadership responsibilities to others, usually someone who reports to her.
4. Finally, the sponsor begins to pull key resources from the project.

I am going to suggest something that many may find risky, but in my experience, you must have an open, candid conversation with your sponsor about the implications of her behavior.

I know that is difficult, but I come back to your attitude. You must see yourself as a technical expert in the planning and management of projects. You need to be prepared to be very concrete about the examples you use to illustrate your concerns. Generalizations will not cut it here. For example, you might need to say, "You had committed to attend the town hall meeting as part of the communication planning, and the stakeholders are expecting to see and hear from you." A vague statement such as, "There is a risk that stakeholders might think you are not supporting the project" will:

- Be denied in the first place.
- Provide no actionable response.

I am asking you to be not aggressive but assertive. Again, *Merriam-Webster's* describes "assertive" as "confident, bold, decisive and forthright." That is the attitude you need to convey.

> "I believe the single most significant decision I can make on a day-to-day basis is my choice of attitude. It is more important than my past, my education, my bankroll, my successes or failures, fame or pain, what other people think of me or say about me, my circumstances, or my position."[1]
>
> *Charles R. Swindoll*

Points to Remember

- Have a way to alert your sponsor about important information.
- Use your sponsor for credibility under certain circumstances.
- Engage with your sponsor to deal with blockers.
- Stay alert to the danger signs.

9

Preparing Sponsors
for Their Role

IN FIGURE 9.1, the project manager is attempting to influence the behaviors of the users of the project deliverables (the actions taken by
individuals to complete the work that comprises their job). Several elements influence conduct, including beliefs, cultural norms, experience, and perception. This is the context we must understand when we
hand off our project deliverables to operations. For example, a project
will not be sustainable after completion if it requires behavior that is
highly individualistic (e.g., make a decision to provide a customer a
financial refund) in a company culture that values command-and-con-
trol (e.g., in the past only senior managers could make those decisions).
Any person who was not asked to provide refunds would be highly
suspicious of any requirements for them to make that decision in the
future. As you can imagine, the employee would want ironclad assurance that there would be no negative repercussions.

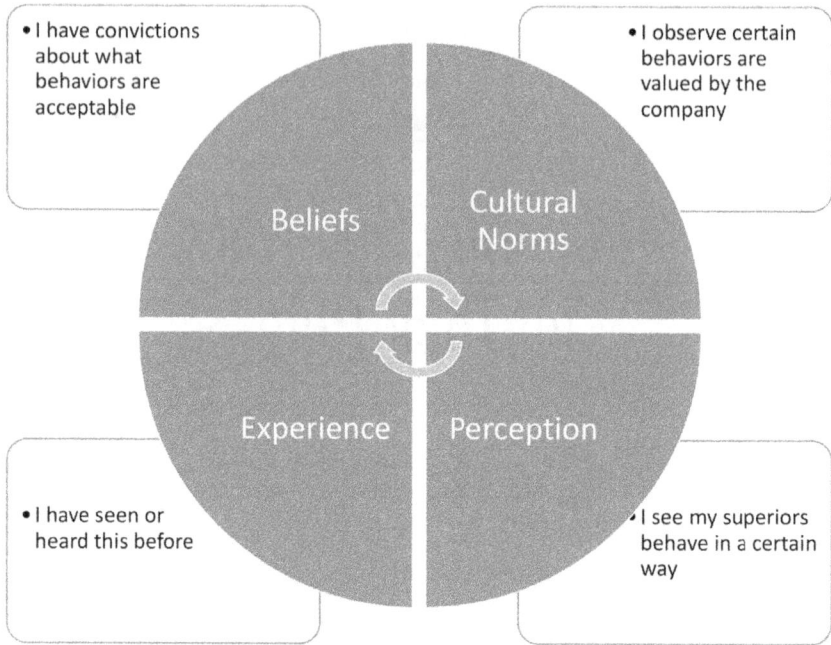

- I have convictions about what behaviors are acceptable

- I observe certain behaviors are valued by the company

Beliefs

Cultural Norms

Experience

Perception

- I have seen or heard this before

- I see my superiors behave in a certain way

Figure 9.1: Influencing Behavior Is a Complex Process with Several Important Aspects to Consider

Determine Where and How Your Sponsor Can Help

In preparing sponsors for the project, we need to think of distinct areas where their help can be important to the success of the project:

- What actions are required from the sponsor to demonstrate commitment to the change?
- Are there any risks from the risk register that require our sponsor?
- Are there certain messages from our communication plan that require authority to deliver?
- What actions require our sponsor to address if there is a lack of readiness on the part of the business for our project deliverables?

Unfortunately, as project managers, we have very little impact on people's beliefs and experience. And we need to understand the cultural norms that influence people so that we can be sensitive to those norms as we prepare operations for the project deliverables.

> **Culture is a set of norms related to shared values and behaviors in a group of people. It defines what the group values and how they should act. If individuals in the group stray from the norms, their peers within the group will give them feedback, without even thinking about it—either directly through words or indirectly through body language—to return to the normal behavior.**

Persuading Stakeholders

Most of the time when we are asking sponsors to get involved, we are trying to convince or persuade them. To understand how people are influenced and how to successfully engage our sponsor, we need to understand that there are principally three ways people are influenced:

1. Authority
2. Technical expertise
3. Relationship

Obviously, the best utilization of our sponsor is to influence through authority. For example, in a project where we were implementing a new trading system for gas traders, one of the key concerns was related to security. Past bad behavior had led traders to give their log-in ID and password to interns so the interns could enter trades while the traders returned to the telephones to capture more orders. As should be apparent to anyone, giving others your corporate log-in information is very hazardous both for the individual and for the company.

Once the new system was implemented, that practice would no longer be tolerated. It may be apparent, but our sponsor, the vice president in charge of all the traders, was the one who had to make it clear that the new system meant changes. He was their boss. As we moved closer to the go-live time, we set up a series of meetings and messages from the sponsor detailing expectations about the new practices. The meetings were part of the strategy because the traders had to see their boss supporting the project and answering specific questions about what would happen if a trader were caught operating in the old way of sharing log-in information.

To influence this group in accepting the new trading system, we relied on two key traders who were recognized by the entire team and very good at their job. These two individuals were at the director level and reported to the sponsor.

In other projects, it may require a different authority to deliver the message, for example human resources, but in that case, the sponsor can reach out to a peer in that department to request assistance.

In a completely different project, the relationship form of influence was required to support the project. The project was building a pipeline that would require landowners to provide a right-of-way over their property. As I am sure you can imagine, the landowners had several concerns, not the least of which was the safety in the construction and operation of a pipeline. In that project, we identified three landowners who were seen as leaders by their neighbors and who had the confidence of the community that they would not place themselves or their friends in jeopardy. Those three individuals became a committee that reviewed all the plans and procedures utilized by the company to provide safety and security during both the construction and the operation of the pipeline, and they became a powerful voice in the community. Admittedly, some landowners remained skeptical, but when their neighbor leaders felt comfortable with the project, a great many of them accepted it.

Building a Leadership Plan

It may seem obvious, but the figure 9.2 identifies the type of executive support you need. It is your job to help your sponsor provide leadership by building a leadership plan to supplement the communication plan.

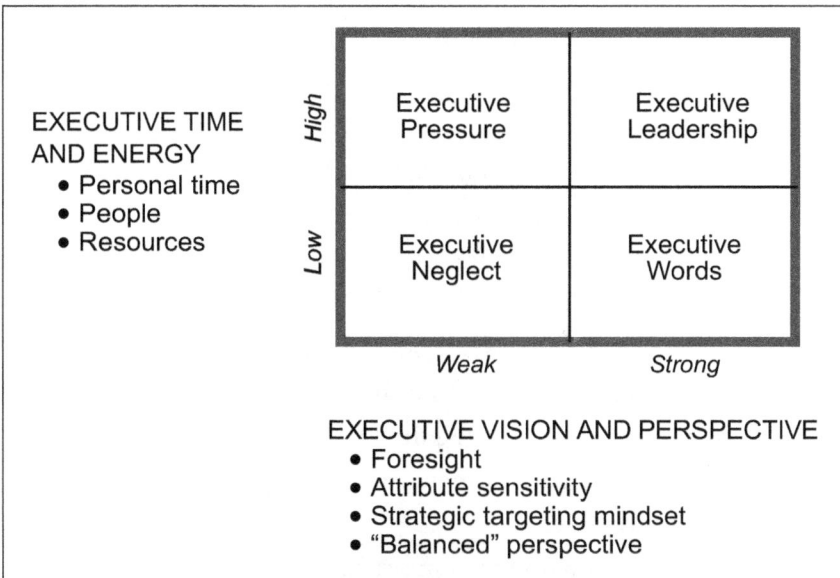

Figure 9.2: Effective Leadership Requires Time and Energy as Well as Vision and Perspective

In a leadership plan, it is best to develop answers to the following questions and collaborate with your sponsor to get alignment:

- From the communication plan, what messages require authority to be delivered?
  - From those messages, which leader would be most appropriate to deliver the message?

- What would be the best forum or medium for the delivery of this message? Please don't just default to an e-mail message!
- What information or preparation is required by the project team to support this business leader?
- Is there a way to get feedback on the message to ensure it had the desired effect?
- Is there a proper timing for this communication to be successful?
- Finally, do any company protocols have to be followed for this communication?

- From an assessment of the impact of changes created by the deliverables:
  - Who will be responsible for the changes to be implemented successfully?
    - Do we know their level of support for the project?
    - Does the sponsor need to engage this person or these people to gain their support?
  - What actions will be required of this leader to demonstrate commitment to the change wrought by the deliverable?
  - What information or support can the project team supply to assist leaders?
  - Is a proper timing required for the action to be successful?

- From the risk register:
  - Are any risks identified that need someone from the leadership team to assist in mitigating them?
  - What would our sponsor suggest related to the risk and the actions required to mitigate that risk?

- Will this activity reduce the likelihood of the risk occurring, or will it reduce the negative impact if it should happen?
- What information or support would that leader require from the project team?

Points to Remember

- Identify how and when a senior manager is required, and prepare your sponsor for that role.
- Remember that technical expertise is more persuasive than authority in many situations.
- Build a leadership plan to complement your communication plan.

10

Clearly Establishing the Communication Channels to Stakeholders

WHEN MOST OF us think about ensuring the success of our projects, our bias leads us to go immediately to defining the scope correctly, having a complete Work Breakdown Structure, or managing risks. The Project Management Institute (PMI®) recently published the Pulse of the Profession™ report on successful projects. The Pulse study, based on research from Forbes, PricewaterhouseCoopers, and Towers Watson revealed that the most crucial success factor in project management was actually effective communications to all stakeholders. The study also concluded that a stunning 56% of the dollars at risk were due to ineffective communications. So what can you do as a project manager to avoid these problems? I would suggest that you work with your sponsor to build the channels of communication. You may need to "educate" sponsors on some of the concepts in this chapter, but I will get to that near the end.

Communications: It's All About Perception

Much of our understanding comes from our perceptions. Every time you communicate with people, your project team, stakeholders, or anyone else, you must keep their perspective in mind. Figure 10.1 illustrates how perspectives influence people's understanding. Before you communicate anything to anyone, analyze your audience. Ask yourself the following questions:

- What information do people need?
- Does the message I'm sending communicate a particular feeling or attitude? (You may need to alter the tone depending on how you answer the question.)
- What is the best media (e.g., one-on-one meeting, town hall, e-mail) for delivering the information?
- Who is the best person to deliver the information?
- How should I deliver the message?
- When should people receive the information?
- How will I receive feedback on how people react to the information?

A basic communication model demonstrates that perception comes from our experiences, culture, word choice, values, and judgments. We use all these elements to encode and decode messages, and communication occurs only when the circles overlap. Otherwise, misunderstandings are inevitable.[1]

Recently, I had a colleague who was in a tough situation that all project managers find themselves in at one time or another. The project was coming into the final months. Things had gone very well up to that point, but the final few months threatened to undo all the goodwill that had been built up over the previous 18 months. While many of the issues that surrounded the project were more complex than is

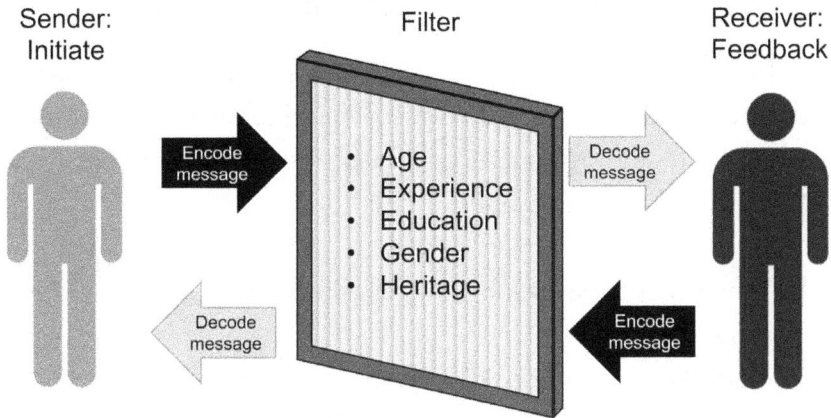

Figure 10.1: A Simple Communications Model

necessary to detail here, there was a basic flaw in the communications strategy. My colleague as the project manager had fallen into the habit of communicating with the business users through e-mail only over the last few months. As most of us know, between the tremendous amount of e-mail (much of it unnecessary) that everyone receives, coupled with spam, many people will ignore e-mails after a while. And that is what happened to this project. My friend had to go regroup and return to a more robust set of communication activities to help the project finish with the amount of goodwill they deserved based on the terrific job they had done.

Engaging Your Sponsor in Communication Planning

All of us know that we need a communication plan, and that starts with a stakeholder analysis. My suggestion is that you draft your initial answers to the following questions and then review the draft with your sponsor. Here are the questions:

- Who needs to be informed or consulted regarding our project?
- What does this stakeholder already know about the project?
- Do we need to consider any sensitivities or political aspects in engaging with this stakeholder?
- What might the stakeholder dislike about the project?
- Do we need to overcome any obvious barriers (e.g., time zones) to successfully engage this stakeholder?
- What is the purpose of the communications to this stakeholder?
- What will we need to communicate? And how frequently?
- What is the best channel for delivering information to this stakeholder?
- Who needs to be responsible for the content and delivery of the information?
- How can we receive feedback from this stakeholder over the course of the project?

Many of these questions may seem obvious, but a few deserve a closer look. For example, related to sensitivities or political aspects, I learned something very interesting about a stakeholder only through the review with my sponsor as we were working to establish a Project Management Office (PMO) in the company.

It seems that one of the key executives who was identified as a stakeholder had tried to implement a PMO a few years earlier. The initiative had not gone well and was eventually abandoned. From a political angle, my sponsor was very concerned that this executive would be very critical of our efforts and would attempt to find any flaws or weaknesses in our project. This reason was simple: He did not want the executive that was my sponsor to succeed when he had failed. I would never have known that if I had not reviewed my stakeholder analysis and communication plan with the sponsor.

As a result, my sponsor and I developed a very detailed engagement plan, beyond just communications, for this stakeholder. It also alerted me to the fact that I needed to keep my sponsor well-informed about any issues that might arise during the project that would be visible to this executive. My sponsor was concerned that the other executive would attempt to blindside him if there were problems. The goal of the other executive might be to make my sponsor look uninformed and leading a project that was out of control. Remember the discussion in Chapter 1 about politics at this level.

Sensitivity Analysis

All these groups will have some sensitivities that you and the sponsor will need to consider when developing the communication and engagement plan. For example, in a project I was leading that implemented a customer relationship management (CRM) system, the sales professionals had a sensitivity regarding any system that seemed to add a layer of bureaucracy to the tough business of selling goods and services. They rightly complained and followed up with a statement something like, "What would you rather I do, sit around all day entering information into a computer or be out on the street selling products?" The answer to that question is obvious, but if the sponsor and project manager do not take that into account, the project will run into some serious resistance later on as they try to implement the new CRM.

In the same project, my sponsor talked to me about a three-month delay in some of the implementation activities. I was quite surprised because sponsors usually are pushing us the other way—to finish faster. My sponsor could not tell me at the time, but the reason became apparent a few weeks later when the company announced a major reorganization. My sponsor knew what was coming, but she was not allowed to share the information with me. However, that knowledge allowed us to revise our plans for activities until some of the issues related to the new organization were at least a little settled.

The point is this: Working with your sponsor can help you understand and prepare for the sensitivities related to stakeholders that you might not be aware of as you plug along in the project. During your stakeholder review, ask your sponsor to be as specific as possible in alerting you to sensitivities that may be above your pay grade to know about.

Purpose of the Communication

Another important consideration when you are developing your communication and engagement plan, is to work with your sponsor to recognize the importance of having a purpose for each message—particularly those messages that have a purpose in persuading people to act or think in a specific way.

When we communicate to others during a project, we typically have three purposes in mind:

1. Inform them using facts and data
2. Teach them new skills or knowledge
3. Persuade them to think, act, or feel a particular way

We still have to be aware that, when we seek to inform people, we do not want to get into the habit of giving a weather report. As mentioned previously, that was the term one of my mentors used to describe reports to stakeholders that really did not provide any tangible information beyond "sunny and clear" or "dark and cloudy." The point is that a weather report that just repeats over and over again the status of the project will ultimately be ignored by stakeholders. If there is nothing meaningful to report, then do not send a message at all.

Of course, your sponsor is a different stakeholder. If the sponsor wants a weather report every week, by all means give it to him. Just do not send that sort of report to everyone.

Most of the time, when we send an important message, we are seeking to persuade the reader how to think or act. Think back to your own experience: If you are persuaded by someone, at the highest level there are usually two reasons:

1. They have authority over you, or
2. The person delivering the message has a technical expertise that you recognize and appreciate.

Both points of persuasion are areas where your sponsor can help you.

Authority and Technical Expertise

There are messages and information that must come from your sponsor. It will be important that people see tangible evidence that the sponsor is engaged and supportive of the project. And sometimes you must send a message that the changes wrought by the project are not optional.

One example is that of the new trading system being implemented for gas traders. As previously explained, in addition to persuading the traders to use the new system, we also needed to put an end to the bad business behavior of traders giving the order ticket to interns, who would actually enter the trade into the system using the traders' log-in information. In this situation, the message was that this business practice would end with the new system. Going forward, traders were forbidden from sharing their user names and passwords with anyone. That message could only come from the sponsor, a vice president to whom all the traders reported. The message that there were no exceptions had to come from him as the authority figure.

Other messages had to come from the directors and managers who supervised these traders because they were the authority figures who actually supervised most of the work. However, even in this situation, the sponsor had to ensure that these management people understood that he expected them to hold their people accountable for implementing the system successfully.

In this same project, we also had to use the technical expertise of certain people to persuade the traders to accept the new system and the changes to workflow that accompanied it. To persuade the traders that the new system was really good and would help them make more money, we employed a couple of very successful traders. We kept them informed about everything that the project was doing and asked for their input at certain times when decisions were being made. When the time came to do some demonstrations of the system, we made sure these super traders were involved and prepared to help us answer questions from the larger audience.

As you can imagine, when the traders saw their peers, whom they recognized as really good at the job, answering questions and demonstrating the system, most of their concerns evaporated. The technical approach had changed their way of thinking and began to get them excited about the new system.

Mix the Media

In the project just described, we used a variety of media to open channels to the stakeholders. The message from the vice president about the trade entry change came during a town hall meeting. The company had two major hubs of operations, so the town hall was conducted in both locations.

The communication from the directors and managers came through their normal staff meetings. We developed a series of slides for them so that we could ensure the consistency of the message. We also reviewed the slides with them to make sure any of their questions were answered before they had to deliver the information. If possible, we had someone from the project team there to provide assistance if they needed it.

Finally, the demonstrations of the system where the technical expertise of top traders was used occurred during a lunch-and-learn session.

We also published a newsletter that was placed on their desks about every two weeks. You may be thinking that seems rather "old school," but please consider this: People so rarely see printed information anymore that having a document in their hand was pretty unique, and our feedback was that people actually read it!

Points to Remember

- Perception is critical to creating successful communication channels.
- Be sure to engage your sponsor in the communication plan in the appropriate ways.
- Don't forget to recognize any sensitivities in the audience.

11

Creating Internal and External Communications with the Sponsor

YOUR SPONSOR CAN be a valuable resource when it comes to communicating internally and externally. However, you must prepare a game plan for best utilizing the sponsor. In Chapter 9, I discussed the use of authority to influence people, and that is the lever you will want to apply for various communications.

Conflict and Communications

During a project, it is normal to find yourself in a conflict situation. You may find yourself in a conflict situation for a lot of reasons, such as:

- Some people try to get what they believe to be their needs met in nonproductive and indirect ways.
- Others do not recognize or understand what they are really struggling with relative to the project.

You can deal with conflict in several ways:

- View the conflict as a competition that leads to you and the other person trying to win.
- Avoid the conflict in a variety of ways such as concession, but that usually does not end well for the project.
- Collaborate with the other person in an attempt to find a solution that you can live with and that the other person can agree to so the project can move on.

In any case, you need to have a conversation with your sponsor on how to best handle the conflict. In my experience, most people start with a position of competition where they want to win.

> Conflict, when taught in terms of conflict resolution, is commonly defined as "when two or more parties perceive that they have incompatible goals and therefore seek to undermine each other's goal-seeking capability."
>
> *Professor Lorelei Ortiz, PhD*

A real key to resolving conflict is listening carefully. That may seem counterintuitive because our first reaction is to prepare our arguments and get ready to go into battle. However, over my years of working in projects, I have noticed that the root of the conflict is often that each party is actually seeing the problem differently. Normally, each side is describing a symptom they either see or expect. So listening carefully will help you uncover the issues as the other side perceives them. From there, the next step is to focus the adversaries—and you may be one of them—on finding a common solution for the problem/issue.

Let me give you an example from my own experience. The project I was asked to deliver was to build a Project Management Office (PMO) for a global oil field services company. The PMO would support and coordinate new product development across multiple service lines with a goal of reducing the amount of time from concept to market. My sponsor for the project was the senior vice president of technology. As we began to work on pulling together the PMO, my sponsor began to get serious resistance from the president of one of the most profitable divisions. This president was a key stakeholder, and if he waivered or refused to support the PMO, it would fail.

My sponsor and I arranged a meeting with the president to explain what we were doing and how it would improve time-to-market for his division. That was our first mistake. I immediately saw the resistance that my sponsor had seen. The president began to talk, at length, about how he held his people accountable, and he did not need this Project Management Office.

This back-and-forth went on for 20 minutes or so, and I realized we were not going to sway him. This was a very senior person who was rarely challenged except by the CEO. So rather than continuing a strategy of trying to convince him, I decided to switch gears and began to ask him questions. I really listened and worked to understand where his objections were coming from. Soon we uncovered the real issue in his mind.

When he heard this initiative would be the "Project Management Office," his mind focused on the word *management*. His interpretation of the office was that our project would create a group that was responsible for building technology that was outside his span of control within the corporate hierarchy. He had confused the word *management* in the title with line management, and he would never agree to that.

Once my sponsor and I understood his need (control and accountability), then we could frame what the PMO was very differently. In fact, we completely abandoned the title (PMO) altogether because we were concerned that other senior management had the same objection, and we just had not heard them say so yet. And to make it clearly fit into my

High

	Compete (I) Win - (They) Lose	Collaborate Win-win
Avoid Lose-Lose	Accommodate (They) Win – (I) Lose

Competition

Low   Cooperation   High

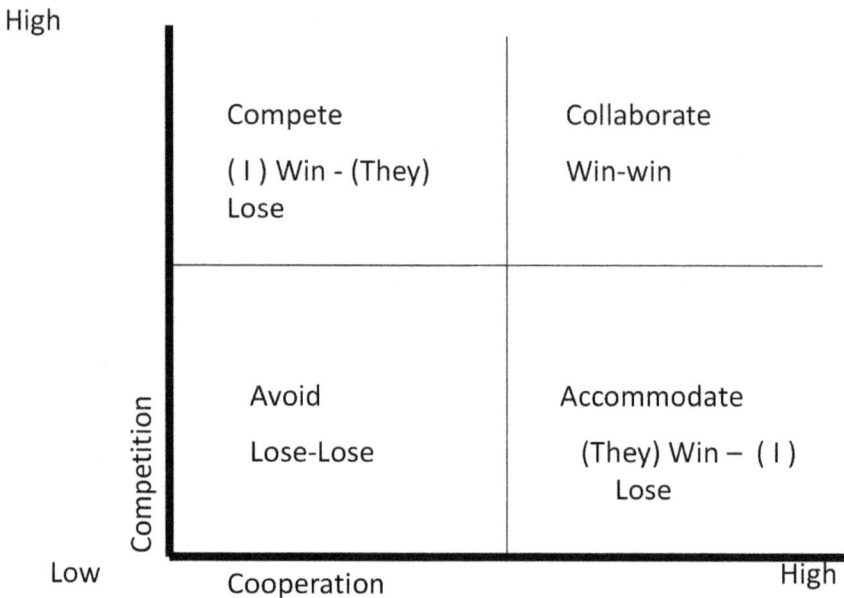

Figure 11.1: Dimensions + Behaviors of Conflict

sponsor's span of control, we ended up renaming the group as Technology Support Services. It really did all the same functions as you might see in a PMO, but the labeling diffused the concerns of the division president, and we were able to successfully complete the project.

Most of the time, the sponsor will ask you to collaborate with the other person to solve the problem. However, while that is the ideal approach, you may need your sponsor to intervene with others in order to motivate them to take a collaborative view.

See Figure 11.1. As you can guess, the real place to aim is in the upper right-hand quadrant.

Four Emotional Skills to Develop

In order to effectively handle conflict during your project, you have to develop four skills. These four skills will serve you well because sometimes the conflict will be with your sponsor and other times you will need to work with your sponsor to solve problems.

First, you must learn to not take the conflict personally. I recognize this is hard inasmuch as, even after many years, this is something I still need to work on. Let's face it, often our projects become our baby, and no one appreciates when someone else tells them that their baby is ugly! However, we need to go back to the beginning and recognize that a project was really sanctioned to improve the performance of a business. When you feel yourself starting to get angry, take a walk and tell yourself that the perceived attack is not personal—just business.

Second, don't make assumptions. In the story I just related, I had made an assumption that the division president knew what a PMO was! Always challenge yourself about assumptions you might be making. A good test might be to ask yourself, "If I walked up to someone in another setting, would they understand what I am talking about?" The assessment of the answer you are likely to get will help you recognize the assumptions you are making.

The third skill is called listening with a third ear. What that essentially means is to put yourself in someone else's shoes and guess what they would understand about your priorities.

Finally, develop the skill of being open-minded about solutions. Others will respect you, work with you more openly, and will see you as rational and reasonable.

Approaching the situation with integrity and in the spirit of resolving the problem goes a long way to solving any conflict.

Presentations to Stakeholders

In making a presentation to stakeholders, the process basically comes down to two parts:

1. Preparation
2. Delivery

In preparing for a presentation, the first step is determining the purpose of your presentation.

> The way you organize the information will depend on your purpose, so make sure you clearly determine your purpose.

Four basic objectives describe the purpose for any presentation:

1. **Advocating:** Convincing or selling a point or approach to the audience
2. **Instruction:** Informing or teaching your target audience something about your project
3. **Inspiration:** Motivating your audience to act on something related to the project
4. **Stimulation:** Stimulating debate or discussion among the stakeholders

So let's take a look at these basic objectives and see how they might apply to a project.

1. **Advocating:** For some of my projects, I have been asked to present to the sales managers and give them an overview of the project so that they can understand why the company is moving in this direction. Here I am selling an idea to a target stakeholder group that needs to understand the benefits of a project. In this scenario, I have to be cognizant that this group sells all the time and that they may be highly critical of my objective, so I must plan carefully. I will also use a technique called preselling as part of my strategy. In presell-

CREATING INTERNAL AND EXTERNAL COMMUNICATIONS WITH THE SPONSOR

ing, I am preparing the presentation and then reviewing my content with a person I feel is friendly toward the project so that I can get his feedback.

2. **Instruction:** Other times, I have been asked to give an overview of the project to the executive committee of the company so they can understand what the project is all about. I would probably choose instruction as my basic purpose because I want them to know the schedule and the business outcomes of the project at a bare minimum. However, I might also cover the Business Case for the project and the overall goals. Here, we want input from the sponsor and ask that she presells the presentation to someone who will give us feedback in a highly charged political environment.

3. **Inspiration:** In other situations, I have been asked to brief management in order to make sure they will provide the support that will be critical for the project's success. In this case, I would choose inspiration as my basic purpose. I want to motivate them to assist me in getting the entire organization behind the project because I am concerned that I will meet stiff resistance at times. Providing information that convinces the management team to back me with their departments will be the key to a successful presentation. Remember, these are the people who supervise those who actually do the work!

4. **Stimulation:** In this case, I might need to make a presentation to a working group to get them to consider possible alternatives for the Working Committee. In these situations, the Working Committee simply does not have time to dig deeply into this subject. Obviously, the presentation needs to stimulate discussion and get them involved in the solution so that the final result comes from the people who know the business, not as a dictate from the project team.

Remember, if you don't know what you have in mind, how is the stakeholder group supposed to figure it out?

For me, the easiest way to determine my purpose is to answer this simple sentence:

"The purpose of my presentation is ..." Please believe me when I tell you that if you cannot answer that question, your audience will not be able to either.

Next, I want to review the stakeholder analysis I did earlier in chapter 6. I might include some of the following questions:

- Who are the key people who will attend and influence the others?
- What do they already know about the project?
- Do I know their attitude about my project?
- Do I have the right credibility to speak to this audience, or do I need to bring someone along with me who has more or better credibility?
- What concerns or questions will they want addressed or answered during the presentation?
- How do they receive information? For example, do they prefer a lot of facts and data, or will they be more interested in how it will affect them?
- Do I know enough about this group's level of commitment?
- Who is likely to dislike my ideas or information and what will they dislike about it?
- Who loses power or access to power if my project is implemented successfully?

The answers to these questions are critical to being properly prepared to present to any stakeholder group. To help answer the questions and to make sure you do a sanity check, I would encourage you to get your sponsor to tell you how they will respond and react to your information. Your sponsor is on your side but will also provide you with the unvarnished truth.

Strategy

The other critical success factor in pulling together a successful presentation is to choose a strategy that will match the audience and the purpose you are trying to achieve. If you watch any of the many shows on television about the legal profession, you will often hear the judge say to one of the lawyers, "Where are you going with this, counselor?" Too often listeners are left with the same problem. They are having trouble following the logic of the speaker, and it frustrates them. So what can you do? The best solution is to use one of some common strategies:

- Chronological (time sequence)
- Big picture/little picture
- Problem/solution
- Question/answer
- Most critical to least critical (particularly if you may run out of time before you can finish)

In many of my presentations, I know that the audience will have questions and that a question/answer strategy would fit. I decide that I will address their concerns head-on and give them the confidence that my project will fill their demands and more. However, I may also review the content of my presentation using a problem/solution strategy or a big picture/small picture strategy. Then I might confer with my sponsor to sound him out on the strategy.

The final three thoughts about strategy are these:

1. **Keep it simple:** This does not mean to talk down to the stakeholders, but remember, they cannot "go back over it" if they miss the point, as they can when they are reading. So keeping the information simple and practical helps to ensure someone does not get lost along the way.

2. **Keep it in perspective:** That is their perspective. Always look at what you are saying from the perspective of the stakeholders you are talking to by referring back to your stakeholder analysis.

3. **Use handouts carefully:** I usually recommend providing handouts at the end of the presentation. That way, people are not shuffling through the pages and not paying any attention as you speak. However, that is not always practical or possible. Essentially, use the stakeholder analysis to determine when to use handouts and how much additional detail they will need to contain.

Build It in Three Parts

The classic format for presentations suggests dividing a presentation into three distinct parts: the introduction, the body and the conclusion. Here is a brief outline of each:

- **Introduction:** In the introduction, you establish your purpose, cover the benefits people will receive by listening to you, and provide them with a road-map or quick listing of the topics you will discuss so that your listeners can follow along.

- **Body:** This follows the strategy you decided earlier and contains anywhere between three to five main points, along with supporting information. It may seem odd to limit the body to only three to five main points, but research has clearly shown that this number comprises the limits of what most people can comprehend while listening. If you want to think about it in some context, think about the last time you went to a social gathering and met a number of new people. How many names did you remember? Most of us would remember only a few. As you finish the main points of the body and before you move to the conclusion, ask for questions.

- **Conclusion:** After you finish answering any questions, notify your audience that you are finishing. Start by recapping your purpose, the main points, and the benefits that you covered during the presentation. Finally, do not forget to thank them for their time and cooperation with the project.

Points to Remember

- Understand the role of conflict and your communications with the sponsor.
- Work to develop the four emotional skills required.
- Prepare well for any presentation.
- Have a clear purpose and strategy.
- Build the presentation in three distinct parts.

12

Using Deputies of Executives Effectively

ONE OF THE most effective ways I have discovered for managing executives who are impacted by your project is to engage with trusted deputies who report to them. A critical factor to consider is that since the deputies report directly to these key executives, they will have greater access than you ever will as project manager. However, you will need the help of your sponsor to make this strategy work. One of the best ways to get deputies involved is to create a Working Committee. This is the best way to get the business involved and to keep various stakeholders aligned with the project.

The Working Committee

In my experience over the years, a critical success factor for any project is for the business to "own" the project. It could be the operations people, the sales people, or the back office support staff. To get that involvement, I like to implement a Working Committee of people from the affected commercial parts as defined in the Business Case for the project. They are the people who will be responsible for delivering business results after the project is completed. These people may come from all areas of the business. For any given project, the Working Committee might come from sales, marketing, information technology, accounting, and so on. After you have completed your stakeholder analysis, you should work with your sponsor to invite key stakeholders to nominate a member for the Working Committee. The people who I would like to see involved are the deputies of the executive stakeholders. Recall in Chapter 6, when we looked at classifying stakeholders. I want to attract as many as possible from the Influencer category who also have credibility with the Authority category.

Whom to Look For

When I am looking for people to serve on the committee, they are usually at the director level in the organization and report directly to a vice president or similar officer of the company. The reason I want these people is they are still involved enough with the day-to-day operations that they know how the work really gets done in the company. Many times, vice presidents have been removed from seeing how the daily grind actually takes place. However, because these people report to the VP, that executive trusts their judgment and decisions.

What the Working Committee Does

There is a reason they are labeled as a Working Committee. They actually do work on the project—but not on the tasks from the Work Breakdown Structure. This is the decision-making arm of the project team. Unlike a Steering Committee that meets once a month or once a quarter for a briefing, this committee may meet once a week. Their job is to consider options presented by the project team and make decisions.

Over the years, I have learned that there is rarely one technical way to address an issue or problem. Most of the time, the technical people on my team will choose what they deem to be the best technical answer. Unfortunately, the option they choose may not also be the best option for the business. My team members may not be in a position to understand the impact on certain parts of the business even if they are business analysts with extensive experience.

For example, in one systems project I was managing, the vendor came out with a new and improved module that the sales team really wanted. Unfortunately, we had been working on the project for several months, and it would be a major change in scope for the project if we now included the new module. On the surface, it appeared we could make the change to the new module with a delay of only a few months. However, when we took the idea to the Working Committee, the accounting and the scheduling people both had a strong reaction to the change. What was not apparent to the sales team or to the project team was that the proposed changes would have consequences at the back office end of the workflow. After a lengthy discussion in the Working Committee, a decision was made to delay the module and include it in a later enhancement to the system.

This was the value of the Working Committee! The business stakeholders made the decision about the change, not the project team. Each of the members of the committee was able to discuss the decision with their constituencies and defend the decision. The sales director was able to explain and defend the decision to the sales team with a solid understanding of the consequences to other parts of the business. The accounting and scheduling people could communicate with their people to demonstrate that the project team and the Working Committee were considering and protecting their interests.

Now take that scenario and multiply it over dozens of technical decisions, and I think you can see that, when the project was finished, we received very little resistance to the changes we were making with the new system.

Going back to the involvement of the sponsor, you will probably require the help of your sponsor to get this level of people involved in the Working Committee. To make these types of decisions, you will need the best people you can get. The problem is that these same individuals are recognized by others as the top technical people in their area so they are probably already working on other initiatives for the business. Your sponsor will undoubtedly need to negotiate with his peers to get those A-level people assigned to your project.

Also recognize that these same people will probably be asked to perform their "day jobs" at the same time. You must also understand that, unless they are seconded to the project, their day-to-day work will always take precedent over the tasks of the Working Committee. When those competing priorities collide, you will need the help of your sponsor in working with their peers to create some space for the Working Committee members to participate.

How to Use the Working Committee

As the Figure 12.1 illustrates, you will need to communicate to the sponsor how you intend to utilize the Working Committee.

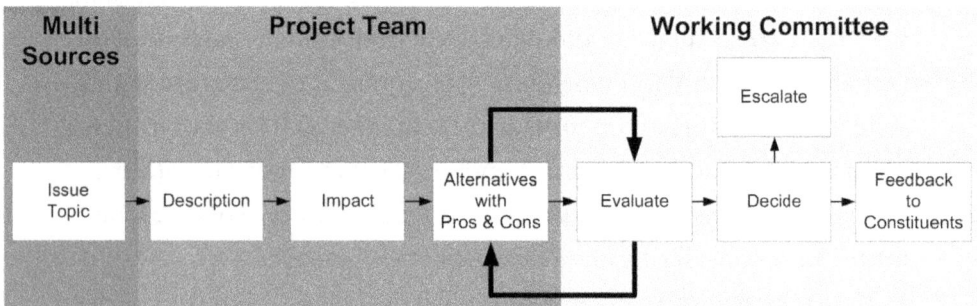

Figure 12.1: The Process for Decision Making within the Working Committee

As illustrated in the earlier example, the Working Committee can also be a valuable part of your communication plan. One of the "duties" of Working Committee members is to keep their constituents engaged and informed about the project.

When I use the term *engaged*, I want to turn back to the module example. When the Working Committee was preparing to make a decision about the new module, what I asked each member to do was to confer with key people in their groups and get their opinion or reaction to the suggested changes. There is a dual purpose in that strategy. First, the Working Committee member is keeping the business informed as to what is going on. Also, the member is asking for their opinion. This can be valuable because often people in the business will recognize consequences that even a knowledgeable member of the Working Committee does not see.

How It Plays into the Politics

Remember from Chapter 1 that the politics at the highest level demand that the sponsor have the project under control. As you can imagine, one of the worst situations for a sponsor, politically, is to be confronted by a peer about an issue and the sponsor was not aware of the issue. You are mitigating most political risks to the sponsor by using a Working Committee.

- The sponsor can use the diagram in Figure 12.1 to explain to her peers how the process of decision making works within the project. She can illustrate, correctly, that it is really the business that makes the key technical decisions on the project.
- The sponsor can also clarify for her peers that the Working Committee member who represents their constituents should

be conferring with those people as part of the input related to decisions.

- Finally, it creates an impression that perhaps the other executive, not the sponsor, is the one who is being surprised by their people in relation to the project.

Believe me when I tell you that, by using this strategy, you are building a strong ally in the sponsor. You have created a model of how the project works that gives the sponsor confidence in dealing with peers. That is huge.

It is huge because the sense of allegiance is an emotional trait, not an intellectual one. When these situations play out and give the sponsor a sense of confidence in what you are doing, believe me when I tell you that the sponsor will defend you during the tough times in the project.

To illustrate from my own experience, I had a project with a Working Committee set up exactly as described here. My sponsor was the chief operating officer of a global software company. We were about three-quarters of the way through the project when one of the division presidents confronted my sponsor about the consequences of a technical decision made for the project. Honestly, it was a complete surprise to me and to my sponsor. I apologized but also explained that we had followed the protocol for decision making exactly as agreed to earlier. I suggested that I needed to investigate and see what happened or what went wrong.

Without going into all the details of my investigation, what I found out was disappointing but not altogether surprising. It seemed that the Working Committee member had not followed the protocol agreed to at the beginning of the project. The practice we had all agreed to was that, when the Working Committee members had to make a decision for the project, they would:

1. Discuss the issue with members of their constituency.
2. Review the options presented by the project team, including risks and benefits.
3. Essentially come to a collective agreement to present to the project team.

As can often happen, the Working Committee member, who happened to be a vice president, did not confer with his people. As is often the case, he was very busy with travel and operational issues and ran out of time. Since the project timeframe required an answer, the vice president gave the answer he thought the team would recommend. Unfortunately, he guessed incorrectly. As can happen in these types of situations, the vice president thought he could tag the project with the failure to implement the correct solution. However, based on the evidence from the investigation, I knew that was not what happened.

Now, I could have thrown the vice president under the bus because that was what he was trying to do to me! However, once I knew what had really happened, I met with the vice president, and we discussed what I had learned. As you can imagine, he decided it was in everyone's (mostly his) best interest to correct the situation with his boss, the president of the division. Together, we worked on an explanation that would let him save face but also clear the project team of any perception of not working in the best interests of the business.

When I reviewed all that had happened with my sponsor, he was delighted. It meant that the division president, someone he suspected was after his job, did not have any grounds for tagging him with a project that was out of control. He also knew that he had some information he could save and use later that perhaps the division president did not have his own house in order if this kind of thing could happen on his watch.

You might read these words and be disappointed that businesses and people could operate this way. However, this is really what happens. You have undoubtedly had something happen to you that you knew was political in nature, but you had no recourse. The approach I am suggesting, using deputies effectively in the project, is a way to help you mitigate and/or avoid those situations. Now you do have recourse but only if you follow the process.

There is always the temptation to take shortcuts when time is precious. Let this be a cautionary story for you to recognize that the use of a Working Committee will take longer in some cases but allow the process to do the job of engaging the business in your project.

Points to Remember

- Use a Working Committee to keep the business engaged.
- Look for people the executive team members trust and rely on for advice.
- Structure the Working Committee to to actually work on the project, not just advise, make decisions and provide quality assurance of the project team's work.
- Recognize the value of a Working Committee in managing office politics.

13

Executing Risk Mitigation Strategies and Executive Sponsor Support

AS PROJECT MANAGERS, we all know that risks will always be present during the course of a project. Many risks will never materialize, and the planning for risks will remain just that—planning. However, a smart project manager will know which risks might require the participation of the sponsor as part of the strategy for managing risks when they do occur. As we know, most project managers must manage three types of risks during the course of a project (see Figure 13.1):

1. Technical risks
2. Business risks
3. Organizational risks

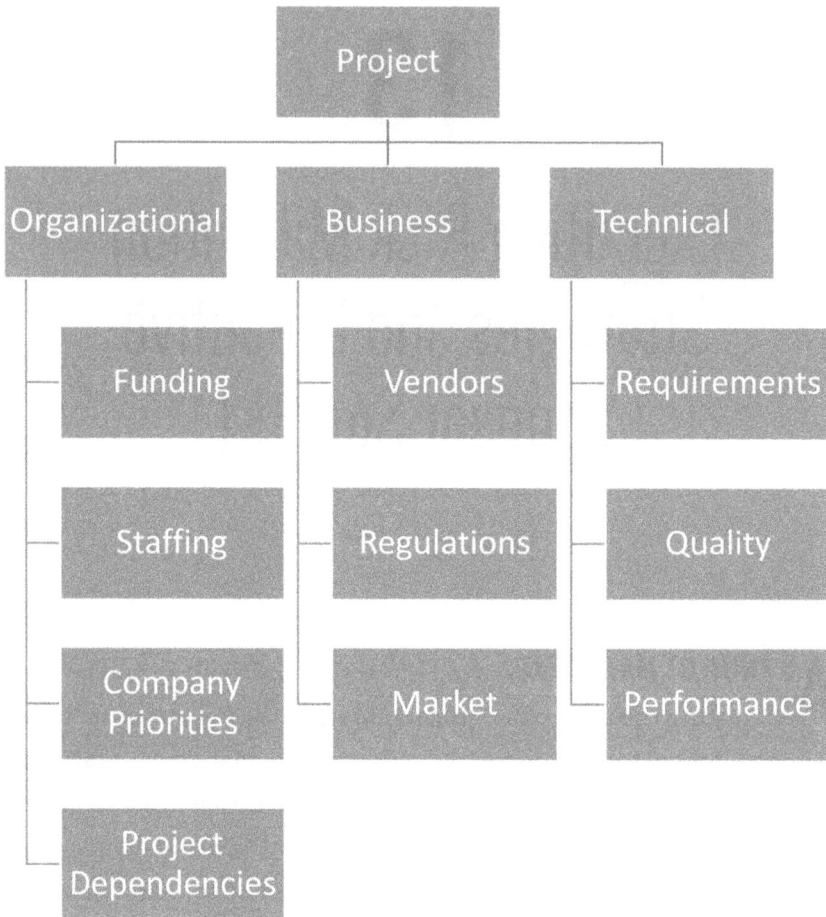

Figure 13.1: Traditional Risk Breakdown Structure

These risks usually come in three categories:

1. Known risks
2. Predictable risks
3. Unpredictable risks

When most leaders think of risks to their project, they move directly to the technical risks. And they usually do a very good job of mitigating those risks because they fall into the categories of known or predictable risks. However, they often fail to consider the two other areas of risk. Business risk and organizational risk are often just as predictable but are usually not assessed or planned for. If these hazards are not considered, they can affect the overall benefit delivered by the project.

Risk Tolerance of the Sponsor

Before you can begin to make decisions about how to plan for risks, you need to consider the amount of risk (the risk tolerance) your sponsor is willing to take in completing the project successfully. Often the risk tolerance will have a direct relationship to the tolerance that the Steering Committee or the executive committee will accept. Often the risk tolerance exhibited by the sponsor mirrors the risk tolerance of the company as a whole. Over the years, I have managed projects for energy companies and have learned that the risks they will tolerate encompass a broad spectrum. Companies engaging in energy-trading activities accepted much higher risks than companies that operated oil and gas fields.

See Figure 13.2. As project managers, we have long seen the classic triple constraint and have also seen more expanded models over the

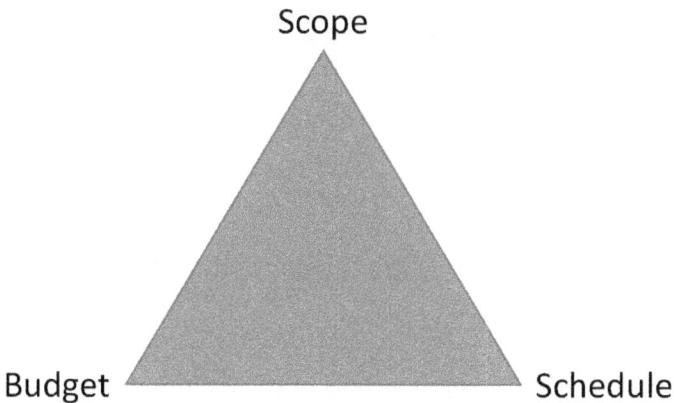

Figure 13.2: Classic Triple Constraint

past few years. However, for purposes of discussion here, I would like to focus on the simpler model in exploring how you engage with the sponsor on risks.

Ask most sponsors, "Which of these constraints is the most important?" You are likely to get an answer something like, "They all are!" In my experience, however, usually one is more important than the others. For example, as part of a discussion with your sponsor, you may learn that actually the project schedule is the most important for the reason that the product your team is developing is very important to the future product line of the company. As part of that future product line, there is a strong desire within the management team to be the first company into the market. The management team believes that there is a significant risk in letting a competitor hit the market first and begin locking up market share. In that case, risks that impact schedule will be far more important to them, and they may tolerate risks to the budget if it means being first to market. In that type of situation, it will be important to talk with your sponsor to determine the protocol for requesting either contingency funds to mitigate risks or additional funds that might be required as events unfold.

In another instance, your sponsor may tell you that he really cannot go back to the executive team for more money. The belief is that the budget is set in concrete and overruns will not be well received. In that case, you need to have a discussion about how to reduce the scope of the project should problems arise while executing the project. The reason for having that discussion now, not later, is illustrated in the next section.

Effective Management of Fear

A wonderful professor I had illustrated the reason for having that conversation early in the project as part of the planning stage. As you can see from Figure 13.3, as the level of fear rises, rational thinking is

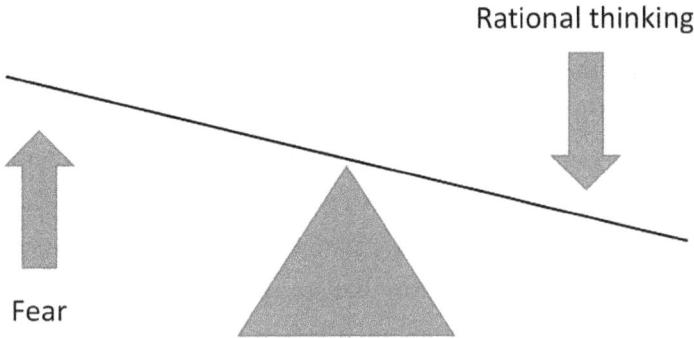

Figure 13.3: Effect of Fear on Decision Making

reduced. If you think about your own experience, you have probably seen this dynamic in action. Working with the sponsor while everyone is in a steady state during the early stages will provide far better brainstorming about solutions. Once in the process of executing the project, talking about budget might be considered similar to requesting a break during hand-to-hand combat. You will not get a good answer.

I would also suggest that you discuss the organizational and business risks with your sponsor. In some of the organizational risks, he will be far better equipped to help you in those circumstances. For example, suppose you are building a team, and some of the team members are being drafted from the business to help. However, they are still expected to pull their weight in their day jobs. In my experience, their day jobs will be their primary concern and could begin to erode the amount of time they are spending on your project. Since you have no line authority over these people, you cannot "order" them to complete their project work. In those situations, you will need your sponsor, who can have a discussion with that individual's manager to work out a solution. You must recognize that risk right at the beginning of the project and get a commitment from the sponsor to help in those situations.

There are other operational risks as you move your project deliverables into operations. I have found that a strong effort in change management is required if the project is to succeed. In an automation project I led, there was significant resistance from the field operators. Let me give you some background so that you can understand how the sponsor and I worked together to solve the resistance problem.

This project involved the onshore operations of a midlevel company in North America. The way they had managed their field assets in the past was to use technicians who had a defined route to check in on the fields and make adjustments to the equipment as needed. The company wanted to build central operations centers in various regions controlled by automation equipment. In the center, the technicians could monitor the performance of the wells and make adjustments using remote control if necessary. If something significant happened, then the center could effectively shut in the well, send one or more technicians to that location, or both. Once the technicians were at the site, they could assess and fix the problem.

As you can imagine, the field technicians who enjoyed a great deal of autonomy under the old system were not eager to embrace the new way of working. One of the biggest fears for the field personnel was the assumption that this automation system would eliminate jobs. My sponsor, the director of research and technology, and I had to develop a plan to engage the managers in each region to make sure that the communication was regular and consistent—that this project was not a project to eliminate jobs. My sponsor had to lead that effort, but, in reality, people trust that kind of information only when it comes directly from their personal supervisor. There was little trust for corporate, which is where my sponsor sat, and I have found that sentiment is pretty common everywhere. We developed a communication for the field supervisors every two weeks and asked them to deliver the message to their people during their Monday morning staff meetings.

While our effort did not eliminate all the anxiety or resistance, it helped tremendously. I believe our efforts allowed the company to meet their business objectives for this project.

Another situation I have experienced during a project is when the budget is suddenly reduced by some arbitrary (in my mind) amount, but I am still expected to deliver the scope of the project without the money originally allocated. This is clearly a risk in all the projects I have led. Therefore, having a conversation with my sponsor early on in the project is important.

I learned a very important strategy from one of my mentors in project management that refers back to Figure 13.2 on the triple constraint. The conversation steers a sponsor to understand that he may demand two of the three constraints, but you are entitled to the third. So in my example of the budget cut, I would refer back to the triple constraint and ask the sponsor to help me figure out how to reduce the scope and the schedule. The focus of the conversation is not that I will not accept the change in budget because my sponsor is probably not happy about that either. In a project that comes to mind right away, my sponsor was the chief technology officer (CTO) for the company. In most cases, you would think you are on pretty solid ground having a sponsor at that level of the company. Unfortunately, he also had a boss—the chief executive officer (CEO). The CEO directed my sponsor to cut the budget on the project. After what I am sure was a lively discussion, the CTO had to accept the directive. And so did I! However, because we had talked about just such a risk during our early risk management discussions, we were able to immediately get into the task of determining how to reduce the scope of the project to match the reduced budget.

Business Risks

I have found it very helpful to engage with my sponsors on business risks as well. I talk to them early on and ask them to help me stay informed if changes in the marketplace might affect our project. Many of these projects take more than a year to fully complete and put into production. A lot can change in a year, but often I am heads-down trying to deliver my project and may not notice that something has changed in the business environment.

For example, I recall a project in which the desire of the business was to be the first one in the market for the new product my project was developing. My sponsor came back from a technology conference where there was a rumor that a competitor was coming out with new equipment that sounded very similar to what we were designing and building. Because my sponsor and I had discussed this very issue several months earlier, we had a plan in place to mitigate the risk of the competitor coming to market first. And very importantly, the sponsor had cleared our strategy with the Steering Committee early on, so we did not have to wait for approval to put our mitigation plans into action. We moved forward and entered the market first with the new and innovative equipment. As a result, the company captured over 50% of the market share.

Although my sponsor was the one who received the kudos for delivering on the project at the company level, he was very grateful for the work the project team did to make it happen. As a result, the sponsor sent the entire team to Las Vegas for the weekend on an all-expenses-paid trip as a way to say "thank you."

It is my firm conviction that the sponsor must be the driver on the business risks. As project managers, we:

- Do not have the visibility on some of these risks early enough.
- Are not in a position to mitigate those risks because we lack the organizational authority.

Points to Remember

- Understand the risk tolerance of your sponsor and other key executives.
- Fear and uncertainty need to be managed carefully.
- Understand that your sponsor and other executives are more concerned about business risks than technical risks.

14

Addressing Scope with the Sponsor

THERE ARE TWO undeniable truths in project management:

1. Scope of the project must be well-defined for a project to be successful.
2. Scope seems to always change during the course of the project.

Working effectively with your executive sponsor can be critical in handling the scope changes that will inevitably occur during a project—particularly one with a longer duration.

Defining the Scope

Over the years in delivering projects, I have rarely had a disagreement with a sponsor on what is in scope for the project. Various documents, such as the Business Case, usually provide input on the scope and shape the project scope.

However, I have often been at odds with my sponsor on what is out of scope. That is why I am suggesting that you work with your sponsor on scope definition. Let me provide an example of what I mean.

Several years ago, my team was implementing a new back office system. The client had learned a lesson about customization from an earlier implementation of an ERP[1] (enterprise resource planning) software, so they chose to do minimal customization for my project. As we were refining the scope of the project, I specifically stated in our Scope Statement that the project team planned to use the standard training package provided by the vendor.

As part of my engagement with my sponsor, I was reviewing the Scope Statement that included what was in scope and what I believed to be out of scope. Imagine my surprise when my sponsor told me that he expected customized training as part of preparing people for the go-live. As you can imagine, this was a big deal for the project.

As you probably know, training for a system implementation generally comes near the end of the project as you are preparing to go live. In this case, after a few classes, my sponsor and I had to sit down to discuss how unhappy our stakeholders were at receiving only generic training on the system. Given the timing, the project team would have been scrambling to build and deliver customized training right near the end of the project. As you can imagine, it would not have been pretty!

To complicate things even more, I had not identified people on my project team who could build customized training on the system. I did have business analysts who I believed could deliver generic training because they knew the system and had the basic platform skills.

So when my sponsor expressed his expectation about training, I was able to have a conversation in which I expressed my opinion that the budget for the project did not seem to include enough money to cover more people—those I would need to build customized training. After I presented an estimate on what the additional cost would be, my sponsor went to the other key executive stakeholders to find out if they would support additional money to build the customized training. As it turned out, the executives decided that the generic training would be enough after all. Basically, they wanted customized training but were not keen on paying for it.

After this process, if stakeholders were to complain about the generic nature of the training, my sponsor could defend the decision and call on his other executives to confirm that they had indeed decided that generic training was enough.

Other Assumptions

The training example is just one situation where an assumption was made about the project. You need to work with your sponsor to ferret out other assumptions so that you can include them in your Scope Statement.

These assumptions can come both from the project and from the business side. For example, recall the system upgrade my project team was doing for installation on oceangoing ships that could be done only when the vessels were in port. To complicate things a little more, the installation could happen only in certain ports around the world, not all of them.

An assumption that the project team had to make was that the customer would give us an accurate schedule of when certain vessels would be in the selected ports. As you can probably imagine, the schedule was fluid. Remember that the company that owns or operates these vessels makes money only when they are in transit, not sitting in port. I worked with my sponsor to set the right expectations with the customers about how their actions might create schedule delays for the project.

Some in our project management community might consider this example as a constraint on the project and could make a strong case for using that term. However you view the situation, as an assumption or a constraint, the important point is that you are working with your sponsor to ensure you are on the same page.

By creating alignment with your sponsor on issues like this, you are far more likely to get the support you need, when you need it, as the project moves forward. And all of these discussions need to happen either before you begin your planning for the project or during the planning phase. Either way, you do not want to begin the execution phase if you have not had these conversations.

Affected by the Project but Out of Scope

In my experience, what I have seen time and time again is that the project exposes poor business practices that are out of scope. I firmly believe that one of the biggest factors that creates scope creep in projects is when the project decides or is forced to address these poor practices.

It is not always possible to know that these poor practices exist until you are in the middle of the project execution. Therefore, I have a discussion with my sponsor during the planning phase about how to handle such situations. I try to get agreement from the sponsor that we will handle these practices in one of two ways:

1. My sponsor will work with her executive colleagues to convene a working group whose purpose is to address the poor practice that the project uncovered. In this scenario, the work is completely outside the scope of my project. It is often the case that the recommendations from the working group will impact the project, but we agree to go through the scope change process if that happens.
2. The project is tasked with making the changes required to correct the poor business practice but with an appropriate increase in scope, budget, and schedule for the change.

No matter which way the issue is handled, the scope of the project is being managed. We are not falling into the scope creep problem because the process has created visibility at all levels.

How to Manage Changes in Scope

All of these situations create a need to change or alter the scope of the project. Here are some ways that I have involved my sponsors in this very important process.

In working through changes in scope, I have found that getting agreement from my sponsor to use the RAPID decision-making model is very helpful. It is particularly valuable when the key stakeholders cut across organizational and/or functional boundaries. RAPID is an acronym (as most model names are):

- **R = recommend:** This is a person who can actually recommend an action or solution based on his line of authority within the company.
- **A = agree:** This person must agree with the recommendation to change scope. In other words, this person has veto power over scope changes and must agree before a change in scope can occur.
- **P = perform:** This is the person or group who will actually perform the work related to the scope change. This is usually the project team but not always.
- **I = input:** This person or group usually has information, data, or some other attribute that allows the scope change to actually occur
- **D = decide:** This is the part I really like about this model. It clearly identifies who has the authority to make decisions on a scope change issue. Particularly in projects where key stakeholders are of equal rank in the organization chart, this

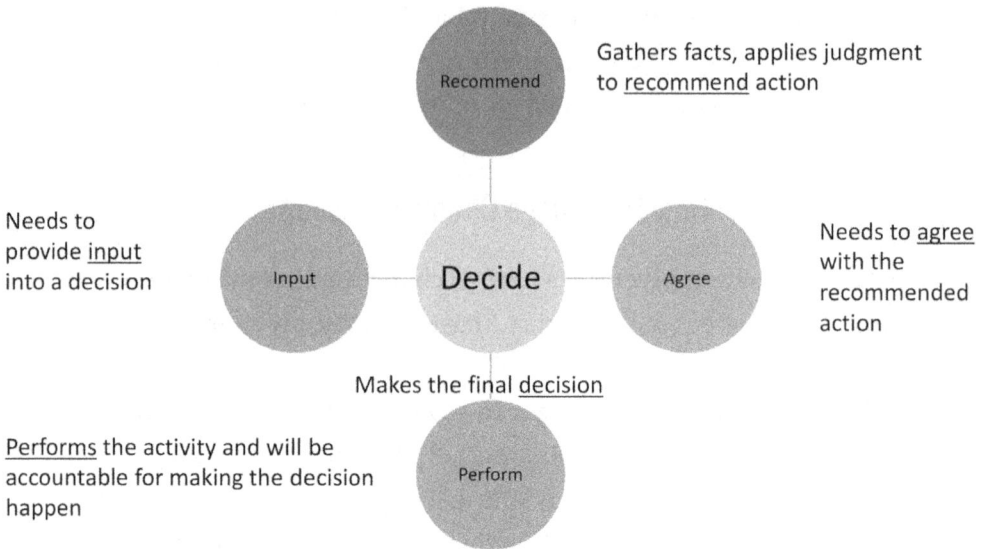

Gathers facts, applies judgment to recommend action

Needs to provide input into a decision

Decide

Needs to agree with the recommended action

Makes the final decision

Performs the activity and will be accountable for making the decision happen

Figure 14.1: The RAPID Method

identifies which one actually makes the decision on a particular scope change.

See Figure 14.1. I find that working through this model with my sponsor makes the whole process of managing scope changes so much quicker—not necessarily easier, but quicker.

Authorization Levels

I discuss who has the authority to approve changes in the scope of my project. In most cases, my sponsor will want to have the final authority but not always. For example, if a change is required because of a regulatory issue, my sponsor might hand off the authorization to legal or to health, safety, and environmental (HSE) to make the call.

Assessing Change Requests

Anytime there is a request for a change, it should come in an official way. An e-mail or short conversation in the hallway should not be how change requests come in. A request may certainly start there, but always have a change request document and a formal set of information elements, including:

- A description of the proposed change.
- Your team's assessment of the impact to the schedule and budget.
- Any impact on the quality of the deliverables.
- Any consequences if the request is rejected.

The real purpose of this prescribed process is not to create unnecessary bureaucracy but to allow you to review the information with your sponsor. I know it may seem cliché, but requiring someone to actually describe in a written request what she wants—and why—requires a rigor of clarity that just talking back and forth can never provide. In most situations, the request will come to you, and you must then package it for a review with the sponsor. And this circles back to one of my earliest comments about not allowing your sponsor to be surprised. With the type of detail you are requesting, the sponsor continues to appear in control and the project well managed.

The nature of the request may also cause your sponsor to convene a change control meeting with key stakeholders. He may want them to consider the request and provide input before a final decision is made. By having all the fundamental information documented, your sponsor can send out the request in advance so that the stakeholders may review it prior to attending a meeting.

In summary, making a conscious effort to collaborate with your sponsor on specifics related to scope definition and scope change will allow you to receive the support you need when you need it. Your sponsor will be in a much stronger position to defend the project from the inevitable assaults that come when a project is under way.

Points to Remember

- Ensure that the scope is clearly defined at the beginning of the project.
- Challenge any assumptions.
- Separate items affected by the project but out of scope.
- Manage changes in scope carefully and formally.

15

Providing Options
and Recommendations
for Key Decisions

ONE OF THE most important parts of developing a trusting relationship with your executive sponsor is providing her with options and/or recommendations for important decisions as the project progresses.

Decision Support Package

As an aid when you ask your sponsor to make decisions related to your project, I have developed a decision support package (DSP) to include all the information I believe an executive sponsor might need to arrive at a decision.

One of the key questions is where to position a recommendation in the process. Most of the time, I like to present the option being recommended by the team right at the beginning. Then I try to build the story as to how the team arrived at that recommendation. In other words, start at the end, the recommendation, and then back up the recommendation using the other materials in the decision support package.

However, I have known project managers who prefer to leave the recommendation at the end after they have presented all their information. My fear in using this approach is that the conversation becomes sidetracked along the way, and we never get the recommendation. That being said, if you have worked with an executive before and you know that starting with the recommendation will not be received well, by all means wait until the end of your DSP to propose the solution you prefer.

Here are the steps in building a decision support package (I will discuss each step in more detail later in the chapter):

1. Provide a purpose statement.
2. Identify any gatekeepers related to the decision.
3. Detail the end results the decision should achieve.
4. Review the options that were considered.
5. Provide an analysis of the benefits.
6. Identify any risks related to the options considered.
7. Arrive at the best balanced choice that is your recommendation.

Now let us look at each step, and I will explain how they help you work with your sponsor. To illustrate the steps, I am going to use an example from a project for a retail chain of auto parts stores that was looking to install an upgraded point-of-sale (POS) system for their stores. The stores dealt with both the walk-in customers off the street and the professional auto repair shops that had accounts with the store. For those not familiar with a POS system, your grocery store probably uses this type of system to scan the items you are buying. The item appears on the store associate's screen so that you can see the cost, the number of each item you purchased, and the tally for the total amount you must pay at the end.

Purpose Statement

Because the sponsor is usually not involved in the day-to-day activities related to the project, it is important to give him context for the decision in a clear and concise way. The purpose of the decision and the definition of the problem or opportunity should also be described clearly.

> **If the decision is time sensitive, you must let your sponsor know when you present your decision support package. Often these decisions take longer than you or your sponsor may prefer, but you are now covered if a delayed decision pushes the timeline.**

In my example, the first phase of the project was to recommend the vendor. I submitted a purpose statement that the team was to recommend a system to the management team based on four considerations:

1. Price
2. Reliability
3. Maintenance costs
4. Personnel costs

My sponsor agreed to the statement and reiterated that the management team wanted an assessment of the total cost of ownership, not just the initial costs.

Gatekeepers

I also wanted to know whether there were any gatekeepers for the decision. A gatekeeper is a critical requirement that must be met for the solution. In other words, there are no maybe's here. We had gathered requirements for the system as any responsible project would do, but I wanted to test another requirement to determine whether it was a gate-keeper. There were rumors on the street that the company might pur-chase another auto parts chain that would increase the size of the company by roughly 40%. I needed to know whether the project team needed to consider that when choosing a vendor.

As is the case in most of these situations, my executive sponsor could not confirm the rumors, as I expected. However, he did say that the team should consider the ease of rapid expansion as one consider-ation in the assessment of vendors.

The other gatekeeper for the project was related to the fiscal year. The company started the fiscal year on October 1, and the management team wanted the system operational at the beginning of the next year.

End Results

When you are presenting options or recommendations to your spon-sor, you must tie them to the end results that the project is meant to achieve. You will want to present an analysis of the choices based on these key end results. Please believe me when I tell you that project managers and executives do not always assess the results the same way.

Options

All the options that were considered should be reviewed at this point in the decision support package. Expressing the options in terms of the important attributes is critical. (See Figure 15.1. Use this matrix to help your team analyze the options.) It will also allow your sponsor to see how the team compared the attributes of the various options. This is the key to selling your recommendation. Seeing the process used by the team to arrive at the recommendation will help your sponsor get inside your head, (Remember when I suggested that the Case for Change was a way to get inside your sponsor's head?)

Step 1: List options as rows

Step 2: Determine important end results and add/remove columns, as appropriate

Step 3: Assign relative weights to each end result in row 9 (i.e. an 8 would be twice as important as a 4)

Step 4: Assign objective 0-100 scores for how option satisfies each end result (best to do this on an attribute-by-attribute basis)

Step 5: Options with the highest scores should be considered

| | 1 | 1 | 1 | 1 | 1 | 5 |
| | 20% | 20% | 20% | 20% | 20% | 100% |
OPTION	END RESULT 1	END RESULT 2	END RESULT 3	END RESULT 4	END RESULT 5	SCORE
Option A						0
Option B						0
Option C						0
Option D						0
Option E						0

NOTES: Of the options you're considering, decide which attributes can be used to help make a decision. You can include as many attributes as necessary. For example, if you're considering multiple vendors, you might use attributes like Cost, Reliability, Company Size, Expertise, Process Familiarity, etc. If you're doing this as a group, make sure everyone agrees what the attribute means. It's often helpful to include a few more words, like: "Process Familiarity—how well does the vendor understand the way we do things at our company?"

For each attribute, assign a relative weight that is greater than zero. In this decision matrix, the range of numbers doesn't matter; it's the relationship between those numbers that matters. For example, if Cost is assigned a weight of 8 and Expertise is assigned a 4, you're saying that Cost is twice as important as Expertise in your decision. Naturally, lower weights are less important than higher weights, and it's okay if multiple attributes share the same weight. In that case, you're saying that those attributes will be treated equally. In group situations, the discussion about the relative importance of these attributes can be very enlightening, and it's a fantastic way to build consensus.

List all of your options. In the example I've been using, this would be the vendor names. Then, for each attribute, assign a score from 0-100 to each option. I highly recommend scoring all options for an attribute before moving to the next attribute, because it's much easier to imagine the attribute, then score each option relative to one another. Of course, if you don't know all of your options yet, this can't be done (for example, if you're using this technique to interview candidates for employment, you may need to score each attribute for the candidate while on the phone). Scores don't have to be perfect, and 0 can mean bad/low confidence/not applicable/failure/etc., while 100 can mean great/high confidence/guaranteed/etc.

Figure 15.1: A Sample Decision Matrix

One trick that I have used very successfully is that I put the winning option as either the first one or the last one. I place the recommended option first most of the time because I want it to stand out from the others. However, I have worked with sponsors for whom I wanted the recommended option to be the last one because the logic they used was impacted more completely.

If the decision must then be approved by the Steering Committee or executive committee, I would recommend that you work with your sponsor to presell the option to key stakeholders. When you talk with one of these people one-on-one, you will usually get honest feedback and/or suggestions related to risks and other factors. If a key stakeholder has a serious objection and raises it during one of these meetings, you and your sponsor have time to figure out what to do about it. If you wait until the presentation to the Steering Committee, that objection in front of all the others may be enough to derail your option.

Benefit Analysis

After seeing the decision matrix, the benefits assessment should be not only easier but also more obvious. In this section of the decision support package, I usually refer to the benefits of each option as one of the following:

- Exceeds the requirements based on the end results or gives the company a significant advantage.
- Meets the needs/requirements.
- Falls below the needs/requirements or provides some disadvantage.

The analysis also should address the weighting that was used to assess the options. Not all of the attributes may be of equal weight, which also colors the recommendation.

Risks Analysis

No assessment related to project management would be complete without a risk assessment. Particularly for the recommended option, you will want to address:

- What could go wrong?
- What is the impact of each risk should that risk occur?
- How likely is each risk to happen?
- How can the project mitigate or avoid any risks that have major impact?

At this point I want to return to Chapter 13 on risks and remind you that, for many sponsors, the business or organizational risks are of greater consequence than technical risks. Therefore, in conducting your risk analysis, pay special attention to these risks even though technical risks are obvious. Also as in Chapter 13, you must build confidence in your sponsor that you can handle any of these risks that might arise.

Best Balanced Choice

In the end, there will be no perfect solution to recommend to your sponsor. Just be certain that you and the team have recommended the right option based on and supported by the data. Too often I have seen people start this process with a choice already in mind. When they start their investigation, they seem to slant the information and data to support their initial solution. Few recommendations will please everyone, so do not try. Choose the recommendation that you can defend based on the data and the assumptions you have made.

Presenting the Options

The other thing to consider when you offer options and recommendations is to choose the best way to communicate them to your sponsor. Everyone has different ways of processing information, so think about how they receive information best. Do they prefer to:

- Read it, then write out everything they need?
- Hear it, then arrange a face-to-face meeting to give them what they need verbally?
- Use numbers, then have you quantify what you are suggesting and put it into spreadsheets?

I have had sponsors who represented all of these approaches. In one project, my sponsor needed to read information and let it soak in before he was ready to talk to me about the decision. I have had others who really did not read much at all, and if they did, the reading had better be short and sweet. These sponsors were the ones who much preferred to sit down with me and verbally go through the information so they could ask questions and seek clarification if they needed it. Finally, in a project I led that was the implementation of a new credit card system, my sponsor was from internal audit. At the risk of stereotyping, I have to say that, for her to understand my requests, I had to illustrate the information using spreadsheets, charts, and graphs.

The point is that you need to present a decision support package in a way that allows your sponsor to make an informed decision. Following the guidelines in this chapter will go a long way in helping you build a strong relationship with your sponsor to get the support you need when you need it.

Points to Remember

- Create a decision support package.
- Use a process to make the decision.
- Present the options considered in making the decision.

16

Communicating Problems and Issues with the Sponsor

ONE OF THE most difficult tasks in project management has to be telling your sponsor about problems and/or issues related to the project. Whenever that happens, the palms of my hands become sweaty, and I breathe with faster, shallower breaths. However, I have learned that while you cannot change your body's response to the situation, you can plan and act so that you can feel confident going into that situation.

Let's start with a reminder from earlier in the book: Never let your sponsor be surprised by a problem or issue. There are political consequences to both of you if your sponsor does not know about a problem when another executive approaches him.

Predetermined Escalation Process

One of the best strategies for engaging your sponsor in problems is to have a set of predetermined steps in place to handle issues that cannot be resolved using consensus. It does not have to be complicated; in fact it should be fairly simple. It is much easier to get your sponsor and other senior management to agree to an escalation project at the beginning of the project. At that point, everyone is still looking forward to the wonderful benefits of the project, and the political aspects have been put aside for a while. And if you do not take the time to establish this at the beginning of the project, you may find yourself in the situation that a colleague of mine experienced during a difficult project.

Several years ago, a fellow project manager came to me for advice. He had a problem that had his project completely stalled and in danger of failing if he could not resolve it. In simple terms, he had a technical issue that affected two key stakeholder groups. However, they could not or would not agree on a solution. When I asked the project manager how he was attempting to resolve this problem, he said through meetings with the key stakeholders. I asked him how many meetings he had conducted to resolve the issue, and he responded that he had already had eight meetings with no resolution. Seriously, eight meetings! When I asked him about getting his sponsor involved, he responded that he did not really know how. In the meantime, his project was in a death spiral.

As a rule of thumb, I set a ground rule for my projects that we will have three meetings to discuss an issue or problem. If we have not solved it, the problem will be escalated to the sponsor. I recommend that you suggest an escalation process right at the beginning of the project and get your sponsor to agree.

My escalation process usually consists of four steps:

1. "We know there is a problem and have a plan to fix it."
2. "The project team is working on plan B to keep the project on schedule if possible."
3. "I will keep you informed on progress, and you will not be left in the dark should you be asked a question about the problem."

4. "I need your support while we fix the problem."

Finally, if I need to get the sponsor involved in solving the problem, then I will provide her with an overview that:

- Defines the problem from each stakeholder's point of view.
- Identifies the option that each stakeholder sees as the solution and the risks associated with that option.
- Includes input and/or recommendations from the project team.

Also, if the sponsor needs to discuss the problem with other senior managers, I will work to help build the message. My goal is to keep the message balanced and as positive as possible.

Probably the most important aspect of handing off an issue to the sponsor is to alert her if an answer or decision is time sensitive. Despite what you might think, the wheels of decision making grind slowly in most companies. I remember a project where my sponsor had to get the decision blessed by the CEO before we could act. You would think that a CEO could make a decision, and we could move on. However, it took the CEO three months to finally provide an answer to my sponsor! As you can easily imagine, that amount of time pushed the project timeline considerably. However, because my sponsor understood the effect on the schedule, he was able to deflect any criticism of the project's delay with a politically acceptable response.

Using a Root Cause Analysis to Explain the Issue or Problem

In working with your sponsor on issues or problems that have occurred, I have found it very important to conduct a root cause analysis as part of preparing to address the issue. My rationale for that is simple—symptoms!

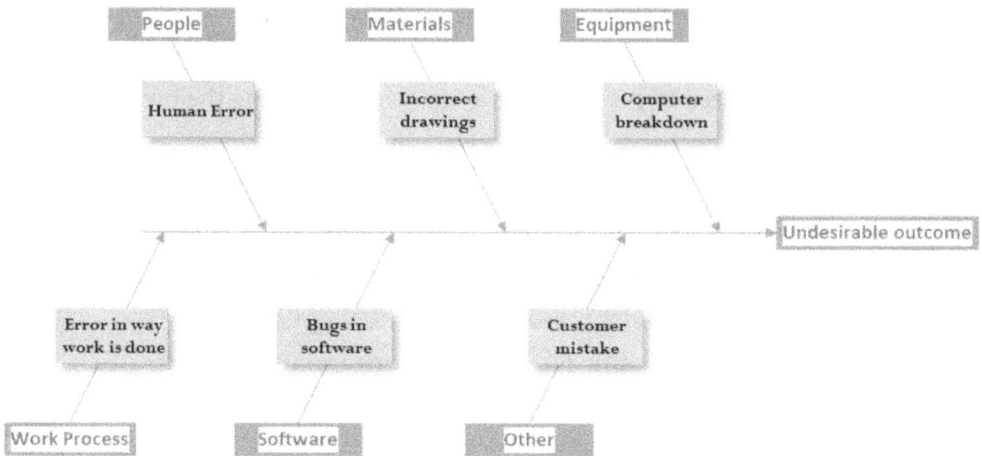

Figure 16.1: Sample Root Cause Analysis

Due to the perspective of stakeholders (often based on their functional roles), they are often reacting to symptoms of the problem. It is very hard to develop consensus if people perceive the problem differently. One of the very useful tools in root cause analysis is the use of the fishbone diagram (also referred to as a cause-and-effect diagram).

Figure 16.1 demonstrates a root cause analysis we did on a project where the team was building models and transferring them into the maintenance system of the vessel. When the client reviewed the models after the transfer, parts or sometimes sections were missing. The resultant rework was causing some delays. However, if the issue was something other than human error, getting the modelers to rework was not going to solve the problem.

In reviewing the problem/issue, it is important to recognize what is being affected. There needs to be a general recognition of four types of issues/problems:

1. Performance (operational)
2. Positioning (strategic)

3. Visible (aligned to results)
4. Invisible (aligned to impact)

You want to be able to describe the event or occurrence using facts, including any data related to the failure. Gather data and create a timeline of events leading to the failure, if possible. Determine how frequently the failure event has occurred and specifically which business process was affected. Finally, identify the exact time and location of the failure event as part of the data gathering.

It is important to ask why at each step and determine what may have caused that step. Then you are ready to create your fishbone diagram.

The fishbone diagram is used in several industries in the attempt to solve problems, prevent accidents, or control quality. The primary goal is to identify factors and outcomes in order to identify which actions or conditions need to be changed to prevent a similar occurrence.

The sponsor may need this background information if another executive complains that an issue is not being handled properly. Often the complaining executive's opinion is based on data given to them by one of their trusted lieutenants. This is where perspective collides with the politics in the organization. Your sponsor will have your background material, which allows him to support the project team with hard data and analysis. That type of information is difficult to refute.

In my experience, root cause analysis has also uncovered problems that are outside the scope of the project. Many of my projects were systems projects, and one of the things I discovered is that system projects often uncover bad business practices. With data you have collected, you can make the case that your sponsor has a few options:

1. Hand off the issue to a working group completely separate from the project.

2. Turn the issue over to another executive where it might be more appropriately handled.

3. Expand the scope of your project to include a correction of the bad business practice.

My experience has been that sponsors generally choose option 1 if the issue is within their span of control or option 2 if it must be corrected elsewhere. Rarely do they chose an option that increases the time and budget requirements of the project (option 3).

Building Consensus

If your project schedule will permit, you should attempt to build consensus when problems or issues cross functional lines.

> Consensus is the general agreement among stakeholders in which each exercises some discretion in the decisions and follow-up actions. Consensus usually involves collaboration rather than compromise.

In trying to build consensus, invite the key stakeholders to participate in the process. There are two key success factors to arrive at consensus, and they will be important to your sponsor and other key executives.

First, ask all who are working on the issue to understand the concerns that each group has. Too often, in my experience, people are prone to jump right into debating the solution. Another reason to seek understanding first is related to symptoms versus the root cause of the problem. Over my years of working with projects, the reason stakeholders disagree on a solution is because they do not have a common definition of it. They are actually describing symptoms that they observe because of where they interact with a workflow or process.

After seeking to understand the concerns of each stakeholder group, the next step is to find a common definition for the problem or issue. The reality is that if there is no common definition, there can be no real solution.

When you have followed these steps, most of the time you will arrive at a solution. This will be very important to your sponsor and other senior managers because you have demonstrated that the people who report to them provided input to the solution. As a result, whatever the solution, it will be supported much more enthusiastically. Plus your sponsor has the ammunition required to show how in control he is and how professionally the project is being managed.

However, there will be times when you cannot reach consensus no matter how hard you try. That is when the predetermined escalation process needs to be utilized.

Determining the Corrective Action

Once you have identified the root cause, you must determine the effort required to complete the priority actions. It will be important that your sponsor is at least aware of the issue in case they are questioned by another executive who is aware of it. Normally, I would share the following information with my sponsor:

- Identification of the individual(s) who will be responsible for the corrective actions
- Adjustments in effort required to fix the issue
- Effects of the actions on the schedule for the project

Remember the goal is to give the sponsor confidence that the project is under control and being managed carefully. He may never need the data from the root cause analysis or the specifics of the remediation actions, but it is far better for him than not having it if questioned by his boss or one of his peers. He wants to be able to confidently answer that he has the information, and if the colleague wants to sit down and review the data in detail, all that is required is to check their calendars and schedule the meeting.

Points to Remember

- Have a predetermined escalation plan.
- Use root cause analysis.
- Build consensus for a solution.
- Determine and sell the corrective action.

17

Communicating with Operations Using the Sponsor

IT IS MY observation that very often in projects, project managers lose sight of the fact that the final product or deliverables from their projects will ultimately be transferred into the everyday operations group within the company. In other words, it moves from being a project to being the operating procedure or tool or equipment that people will use every day to help them do their jobs. While many tasks must be completed before handing the project deliverables over to the operations group, one of the most important involves the communications that occur to get the operations group ready to receive those deliverables.

In this chapter, I want to cover why it is important to focus on these communications and when using the sponsor is key to this aspect of communication.

- Never assume that anyone knows anything.
- The bigger the group, the more attention must be given to communication.

- When left in the dark, people tend to dream up information that become rumors.[1]

The first thing to remember in communicating with operations is risk. As project managers, we maintain a risk log, but these risks are usually related to our project. The greatest fear most operations managers have related to projects is that the project team and the project manager will create problems in their ability to run the business. The concern operations managers have from a project really centers on the risk to interrupting or degrading their operating performance measures. It is important to keep in mind that operations managers often receive their bonuses by hitting their operational targets: If they miss them, they usually put a portion of their bonus at risk. All projects create risks, and operations managers know that. Many operations managers have also had bad experiences in the past with projects that have hurt them in a variety of ways, so they are not anxious to embrace any project.

When you begin to execute the communications plan (see Chapter 10), there are some simple guidelines to follow when delivering good news or bad news.

Good News-Bad News

Good News: When there is good news to communicate, deliver the information early in the message and usually with a tone of congratulations. From there you can explain the consequences of the good news and then follow with any additional details that might make sense for the group you are communicating with. For example, when my systems project had conducted user testing with the system and the system passed, I would start the communication congratulating both the users who had volunteered for the testing and the project team members. They had performed a valuable service to the project, and their contribution needed to be recognized in the communication. The communication should also detail the consequences of the passed test as it relates to the readiness of the system to get the other users excited about using the system. Another consideration is the sensitivity of the communication (see Chapter 10 if you have forgotten what the sensitivity means). Based on the sensitivity of the stakeholder group or the message, it might be appropriate for the sponsor to send the message to the operations group. Please remember that the uncertainty of the project is what concerns operations people.

Bad News: My advice for delivering bad news is that it must generally be handled differently than sending good news. When you are sending bad news, it is important to the respect the feelings and previous contributions of those who are receiving the communication and acknowledge them first. Then the writer attempts to "frame" the bad news giving reasons and facts.

> **Framing is defined as describing a situation through communicating in such a way as to encourage a certain perception and to discourage others.**

Yes, it is bad news, but the purpose of framing the situation is that you want the people receiving the information to have the perception that the project is under control and the issue will be fixed.

For example, in a customer relationship management (CRM) system I managed, I had to deliver some bad news to the sales representatives about setting up the CRM. When the systems were reviewed and the current one chosen, one of the features the vendor promised for setting up the CRM system was the ability of sales representatives to upload their contact list into the system automatically. However, after several tests, the project team became convinced that an automatic transfer created too many errors to be useful. They figured out a work-around using spreadsheets, but it was more time-consuming for the sales reps. I knew the sales reps would not be happy about this development, so I needed the project team to prepare all the details regarding why the automatic transfer did not work. I was not trying to sugarcoat the problem, but I needed the sales reps to keep this issue in perspective. I was worried that the sales reps would lose confidence in the system and that my team would lose support from this critical stakeholder group. Also, I wanted to communicate that all the other features promised by the vendor seem to be working fine and that the sales reps would receive all the other benefits when the system is operational.

In this situation, I decided to work with the vice president of sales and one of his key direct reports, not the sponsor. I felt that they were the right people to communicate the news. It was not that I was reluctant to share the news and take the hits that might follow. The purpose in using these key senior managers was to assure the sales reps that their bosses had not lost confidence in the system and so they should not lose confidence either.

In preparing the communications with these senior managers, I had to work with them and share all the information I had. No one likes to deliver bad news, and they were no different. I had to explain the concept of the power base in communications to justify the rationale for having them deliver the message.

Although this example did not involve the sponsor, the basic concept remains the same, and it did involve working with a senior executive. You will find yourself in situations where the sponsor is the right person to deliver the message.

Informing the Rest of the Management Team

At regular intervals, your sponsor will have to inform the rest of the management team about the status of your project. This can be a time that is fraught with potential risks for both you and your sponsor. Here are some ideas that will help you navigate those situations. In this case, you need to write the first draft and then collaborate with your sponsor to refine the presentation.

The first step is to remember that the management team is not interested in a weather report. While schedule and budget are important, they will seek to understand other items, and one of them is how you are going to fix the problems that have occurred. So ask yourself what questions might they have about the project and the issues? If they have heard about problems from operations, what information might they need about that situation? If you have forgotten, remember the politics involved in these meetings. This is a group of highly competitive, type-A personalities who are striving to look like stars to the CEO and to impress one another. However, here are some key points you definitely want to convey:

- We know there is a problem, and we have a plan to fix it.
- The project team has a backup plan to keep the project on schedule if possible.
- We will keep you informed on progress.
- We need your support while we fix this problem.

Establishing the right perception is paramount in this situation. And remember to keep the narrative balanced between the problem and the solution the project is working on.

Your sponsor works with these people all the time, so rely on her judgment about the type of information they will require in order for them to believe what you are telling them. Give yourself and your sponsor enough time to do a few iterations before the actual presentation.

If you will be delivering the presentation, practice several times to ensure your delivery is smooth and polished. Have a lot of backup data and information at hand should you need it. That will demonstrate control and confidence to the management team.

SUCCEEDING WITH SENIOR MANAGEMENT

In presentations to operations and senior management, it is never a good idea to use the words "I don't know." If you are asked a question and you do not have the answer, your response needs to be something like, "That is a really good question, but I didn't anticipate it coming up in the meeting. I will gather the correct information and have it for you as soon as possible." Be very certain you find the data and get it to all those who are interested as quickly as you are able. Your professional reputation is at risk in this situation. You also need to ask yourself. "Could I have known in advance that this question would come up?"

Time-Sensitive Decisions

Another situation we often find ourselves in relates to decisions we need from operations. Many times, the sponsor can make the call but wants to socialize the situation first to achieve consensus. That is a fine way to manage and will provide better support for your project, except that it may put you and the project schedule at risk if your sponsor takes too long to build that consensus.

It is very important to make your sponsor aware of the time sensitivity of decisions and the associated consensus. Give your sponsor clear and concise guidelines about what will happen if the decision/consensus is delayed. Please keep in mind that your project is only one of many priorities your sponsor has—not the least of which is to run the business to reach various targets. Just as you would in developing a realistic estimate for a Work Breakdown Structure, be realistic about the estimated time it will take your sponsor to reach a decision.

Also keep in mind the style of decision making your sponsor uses. In my experience, I have identified three groups in the way sponsors make decisions. They have these orientations:

1. **People:** These sponsors are very concerned about others, want to appear nonjudgmental, and are interested in building relationships. However, this approach can get them overly involved in the strong feelings of others about a decision, and they can lose sight of the facts.
2. **Action:** These sponsors tend to be impatient and want to jump to the answer immediately. That may be good for you as far as your schedule is concerned, but it may cause hard feelings in a stakeholder group because they have not been consulted.
3. **Content:** These sponsors value technical information and test everything for clarity and understanding. They welcome complex and challenging problems, but because they also try to look at all sides of an issue, they can take a long time to make a decision.

Points to Remember

- Use your sponsor effectively in communicating with the operations group, and you will reap real results.
- Work with your sponsor to give good news and bad news in order to keep the issue honest, not sugarcoated, but also balanced.
- Work closely with your sponsor on informing the rest of the management team about your project to keep alignment and support.
- Be clear when decisions are time sensitive, but recognize that politics and complexity often mean that decisions will take longer than you would prefer.

18

Using the Sponsor to Gain Operations Support

FIRST OF ALL, let's review the key requirements for persuading operations to accept the deliverables from your project: expertise and authority. In addition to these absolute requirements, there are two more:

1. Providing operations with any training that will be needed to be successful
2. Communicating how they will be evaluated on performance after implementation

In actual fact, you could almost think of these latter two requirements as two separate projects that run on parallel tracks until the end of the project. See Figure 18.1.

Track 1

Deliverables:
Getting the Technical Elements Ready for Use

Deliverables Ready
and Provided to Users

Track 2

Operations Readiness:
Getting the Users Ready to Utilize the Deliverables

Users Ready: Engage,
Trained, Motivated and
Eager to use the
Deliverables

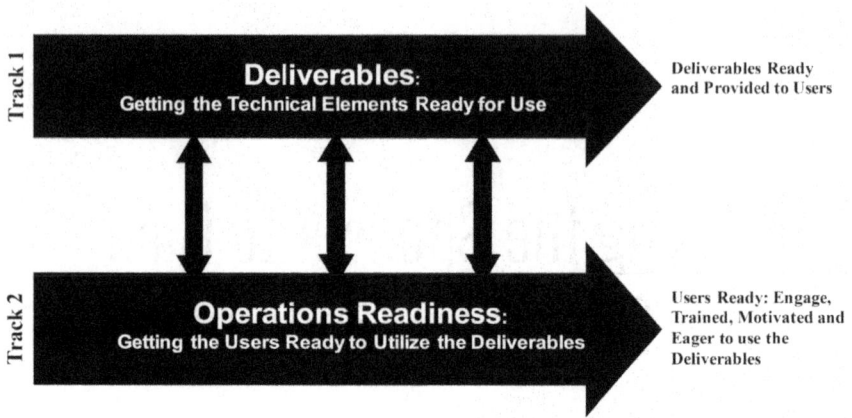

Figure 18.1: Dual Perspective on Operations Readiness

Providing the Training That Operations Needs to Be Ready

Very often project managers take a superficial look at training and ask the question, "What will people need to know to make the project work?" I would suggest that executing the training plan should focus on this question instead: "What will people need to be able to do in order to make the project successful?" Focusing on doing rather than on knowing is a critical difference. It changes the paradigm from a learning solution to a job-related solution. Basically, people do work, and hence the focus on doing rather than knowing. Follow a plan for functional training and competency training during the project execution.

Developing the Content

Here is where your sponsor can help you by recruiting people who are seen as experts and/or highly successful by others in the company—the "stars." You will need training professionals who are experts in their own right, but they often need content help from others. The stars can be the people who do quality assurance and who provide input on the content of training to make certain it is achieving the doing versus the knowing.

However, you will likely need the help of your sponsor to involve these stars. The reason is quite simple in concept but much more difficult to execute. These are the stars in the business, so they are usually involved in other initiatives and not just your project (not to mention that they also have their day-jobs to perform).

> **In business and in football, it takes a lot of unspectacular preparation to produce spectacular results.**
>
> *Roger Staubach, Football Hall of Fame*
> *and successful real estate businessman*

When these people are within the span of control of your sponsor, you may have an easier time recruiting them because your executive can negotiate their participation in the project a bit more easily. I use the words "a bit more easily" because even though their senior manager wants their participation, their direct supervisor will fight hard to resist if at all possible. You have to keep in mind that these stars and their supervisors are where most of the operational work is actually accomplished in running the business from day to day. Their operations supervisor will see big risks in having them assigned to still another initiative.

One way to ease the resistance by a star's supervisor is to work a strategic approach to the situation.

1. First of all, find out what other initiatives the star you want is working on.
2. Second, determine, as best you can, how these other initiatives rank in importance to the business compared to your project.

3. Finally, attempt to determine whether there is a way to reduce their day-job workload so they can spend the time required on your project.

If you take these steps, you now have the knowledge you need to negotiate with:

- Your sponsor initially, and
- The star's supervisor if the sponsor approves.

You can use the same techniques for recruiting people from other parts of the company outside the span of authority of your sponsor, but recognize that those negotiations will be much more difficult. For your sponsor to request time from another executive's team will require that you have a very clear role for the star, along with an accurate assessment of exactly how much time you will be demanding from the star.

In my years of running projects, I have seldom had an executive not offer to support my project with their people. I request the help and they agree. However, if I explain to my sponsor that I will need this expert for two days per week for four months, we have a very different conversation. I am confident you will understand why.

Your sponsor will also need this type of estimate when they begin negotiating with a peer for one of their stars. However, you must provide one other consideration to your sponsor as part of your request for a star—whether in their group or another.

You must provide your sponsor with the risk involved in not having these key people involved in our project. You can explain it in terms of:

- Schedule because without their expertise it will take longer to get activities completed.

- Quality, because the deliverable will not be as robust as it might be if they were involved
- Budget, because without the expertise from the company, you may need to hire a contractor or business analyst with that expertise
- All of the above

This is another area where I think we as project managers must understand the facts of life discussed in Chapter 1. Believe me when I tell you that the senior management did not even think about this factor when they sanctioned the project—at least in most cases.

Delivering the Content

Sometimes these stars have the platform skills that they can actually help deliver the training in the use of the deliverables. In these situations, I have had my training specialist conduct a series of workshops to train the trainer and give them the skills they will need. Your training specialist can help structure the workshops to help them with delivery and how-to knowledge about things like answering questions. In my experience, most of these stars, if they have the basic platform skills, will actually enjoy training others. It provides a lot of positive feedback to them about the admiration and respect that others have for them.

For those stars who do not have the platform skills, you can still use them effectively in the workshops. In this situation, you pair them with a professional trainer, and the star acts in support of the trainer. The professional trainer will deliver the content through presentations or demonstrations. Sometimes trainees will ask those tricky what-if questions that might be beyond the knowledge of the trainer. In such instances, the star is there to answer those tough questions and help the participants understand how to apply the training by utilizing examples that all will recognize.

Either approach takes an enormous amount of planning and co-ordination, so do not underestimate the complexity of either approach. Either you or your trainer will need to develop a detailed schedule to ensure the availability of both your stars and the participants themselves.

Finally, you will probably need your sponsor to help you encourage people to attend training. In my experience, the day-to-day operations always seem to get in the way of training people. Sometimes it is just demands on their time, and other times it is just people making excuses because they do not want to attend.

Using Authority to Deliver Training

When people are making excuses not to attend, this is when persuasion by authority is appropriate. In this case, I am assuming that training is mandatory as part of the handover to operations. If training is not mandatory, be sure to include potential risks in your project reviews with the sponsor. It goes back to the "no surprises rule." For people within the span of control of your sponsor, the sponsor must let managers know that people are expected to attend the training. Even with that, a couple of managers may not pay attention, so keeping a close eye on who is attending and who is not is very helpful. It is very dangerous for your project's success to assume, "If they don't show up, it's their problem." It is not: It is your problem, and you need your sponsor to help.

The sponsor may also need to prod his peers if the people who report to them are not showing up for training. Because there is no line of authority control, your sponsor will have to be the one to handle the situation. If you are asking the sponsor to get involved, you need to provide him with two key pieces of information:

1. The numbers of people who have attended from various departments or groups
2. The contrast of the numbers between other departments and these executives' departments

The comparison of numbers hits that nerve in executives where they want to appear in control in their operations groups. Having data is the best way to break through the resistance to act.

Performance Evaluation and Project Deliverables

One of the biggest obstacles a project manager faces in preparing operations is anchored in the concept of whether the deliverables from a project are mandatory or optional once they move into day-to-day operations. In my work over the years doing systems projects, that has been a real struggle. In most cases, use of the new system was seen by senior management and by my sponsor as mandatory. However, users often saw the system as optional. In my projects, the legacy system had flaws, and people built work-arounds to compensate for its shortcomings. Perhaps not surprisingly, even though the new system would address many of those flaws, people seemed to want to continue to use the tools (usually spreadsheets) that they had developed. I think the reason was they felt more confidence in something they had built versus something that was given to them.

This is another discussion with your sponsor on accountability for actually utilizing your project deliverables after they are put into operations. The key question is really whether the use of a new deliverable and associated business practice will become part of the performance evaluation. As we all know, if people are not evaluated on something related to their performance, they tend to ignore it.

That being said, please remember that if the use of a new process, procedure, or system is going to be part of the performance evaluation, you will need to get the human resources people into the conversation. For most organizations, changing the performance evaluation scheme is notoriously difficult and will require your sponsor to be involved with or supportive of that expectation. Otherwise, it will not happen.

> One of the hardest lessons . . . to internalize is the primacy of departmental loyalties and self-interest over organization-wide concerns.
>
> *Jeffery K. Pinto,*
> Power and Project Management

Preparing operations for the project deliverables is both difficult and time-consuming. However, the effort and time invested in preparing operations properly will be critical to how the project is ultimately judged.

Points to Remember

- The sponsor must be involved in order to gain support from operations.
- Use company stars to ensure the quality of training and perhaps even to engage in the delivery of training.
- Use your sponsor's or other senior executives' authority to guarantee that people attend training.
- Work with the sponsor on whether performance evaluations need to change as a result of your project deliverables.

19

Getting Help with Cross-Functional Issues

GETTING THE SPONSOR to help with cross-functional issues is very important. As a project manager, you will often bring stakeholders together to discuss issues, problems, and content. The sponsor can be a tremendous help when you are unable to resolve the issues and various stakeholders are taking different positions. In my years, these can become very emotional and entangled in the personal relationships of certain individuals, making them even more difficult to solve.

In looking at the way a project manager and the executive sponsor can work together on these issues, I want to remind you of the two critical principles that already were covered in earlier chapters:

1. Never surprise your sponsor.
2. Have a predetermined escalation process in place from the beginning (see Chapter 16).

Your sponsor will be aware that cross-functional issues are a place where she must step in. However, she will need your help to work on the problem and get you the answer that you require. I always let my sponsor know about cross-functional issues if it will require more than one meeting to resolve—which is most of them. At the beginning, I will just give the sponsor a high-level overview of the issue and the strategy for solving it. I will also let the sponsor know of progress in resolving the issue. I will not dump the problem in her lap until I and my team have really tried and failed to gain consensus.

One of the lessons learned over the years in these situations is that the disagreement often comes because the warring stakeholders are not actually defining the problem the same way. Therefore, they will come to different conclusions as to how to solve it. The root cause of this situation has actually eluded the stakeholders; that is, each side is really describing symptoms they see from their perspective. I share that learning with the sponsor so she recognizes that I am seeking the root cause. I want to make certain that if executives from these functional groups bring pressure to implement the solution from their team, the sponsor has a socially acceptable way to deflect the pressure. Few executives will object to a root cause analysis; they just want to be able to tell their constituents they have gone to bat for them and a solution is coming.

Uncovering Stakeholder Perspective

So the first task is to gather data from everyone's perspective. I am trying to gather a timeline of events because I may need to review this with the sponsor to explain the issue. The data I am looking for is:

- Define which part of the business process was affected.
- From each stakeholder group, when does that problem seem to occur?

- How frequently has the failure event occurred?
- If possible, identify the exact time and/or location of the failure event.

To make this process work most effectively, I ask my sponsor's blessing to create a working group that represents all the functional areas affected by the problem. This working group is tasked to review the data and identify each potential cause of the problem and what may have brought it about. I often ask that the working group not be people already on the Working Committee for the project. I am seeking a recommendation from the working group to the Working Committee. In these circumstances, I want the Working Committee making the decision on the recommendation, not the project. As already mentioned, pulling time away from the day job is hard enough on the Working Committee without adding the burden of a problem analysis and recommendation on top of everything else. However, I need my sponsor to approve that strategy and agree to support it.

Obviously the primary goal is to identify factors and outcomes in order to solve the problem. However, there is another motive in approaching it this way: I am getting the stakeholders to focus on solving the problem rather than "winning." Once the situation devolves into a contest, you are putting your sponsor in a difficult situation. Plus, I now have substantial data that I can provide the sponsor if she must approach one or more of her peers to negotiate a solution.

> **One danger in this process is to think, at the outset, that you already know the root cause. If you start from that assumption, it will bias your investigation and cause you to steer toward your preconceived answer.**

If the stakeholders review the root cause analysis and agree to our solution to the problem, the project moves on.

On the other hand, if consensus is not achieved, then I must get the sponsor involved. Because I have been keeping her informed as we attempt to achieve a solution, she is usually not surprised if a stalemate occurs. And that is exactly what I was trying to achieve so that she would not be surprised.

Escalating to Achieve a Resolution

If the cross-functional problem cannot be solved using the process just described, then the issue will have to escalate to the sponsor and other executives who represent the functional groups involved.

In this situation, there are at least two competing solutions and oftentimes more than two. In that case, the project team will have to put together a decision support package for the executives to use to make a decision.

Start with the Purpose of the Decision

You need to clarify the purpose of the decision you need from these executives, starting with the common definition of the problem. The decision should reflect the Business Case or goal that allowed the project to be sanctioned in the first place.

Options Considered

In this step, you want to give the executives a high-level overview of the options considered by the working group and the project team. Also, the risks and benefits for each option should be presented with the assurance of the business integrity of each of those options. Obviously, you should have substantial data to support each option. That will probably include:

- Business processes affected.
- Reports.
- Any other relevant facts and figures.

All the source data collected during the root cause analysis and any other follow-on work should also be available to these executives if they want it.

Finally, you should provide an impact assessment for each option on the schedule, budget, scope, and quality of the project.

Time Sensitivity

Unfortunately, these types of decisions rarely happen quickly in my experience. You should attempt to keep the project on schedule as much as possible, but you must give your sponsor an assessment on the impact to the project if the project takes longer than your ability to juggle will allow. Again, do not surprise them. Have this information at the same time you begin this process.

To that end, I would recommend that your decision support package be delivered to the executives in advance of any meetings to discuss the issues. While it is my experience that they often do not look at the materials until about 20 minutes before the meeting, that should not discourage you from providing it anyway. Often executives travel to other sites as part of their responsibilities, and that may give them the opportunity to do a more thorough job of review than otherwise. I have also had an executive hand off the information to a trusted lieutenant to review in advance of the meeting. The executive will ask for their opinion and ideas.

Presenting the Information

Most of the time, the meeting includes the executives who are responsible for the various functional groups. If that is the case, you will want to plan carefully with your sponsor on the approach to the meeting. You should be interested in knowing the exact role you are expected to play in the meeting. For example, are you:

- Presenting and defending the materials?
- Supporting your sponsor, who will present the materials?
- Supplying answers to questions that come up?

Also, be clear with your sponsor about the goal of the meeting. Are you there to just share information, or are you trying to motivate them to act in some way?

Also review the information on listening styles from Chapter 7 to assess who uses which style in most cases. If you are not certain, review the listening styles with your sponsor and get her opinion.

Handling Questions

When you work with executives and they ask you questions, the first thing you must do is understand the type of question because it will influence the way you answer. Let me explain in more detail:

- **Direct question:** This is probably the type of question you most often think of. They are simply asking you for information, and they expect information or data in return.
- **Summary question:** This question often begins with a phrase like, "Are you saying?" In this case, they are putting what they hear in their own words and seeking clarification that they are hearing you correctly.

- **Logic question:** This question is challenging the logic of the facts and/or conclusions in the presentation or supporting materials. Basically what they are saying is that it does not add up to them. Resist the urge to become persuasive in answering this type of question. Simply lay out the facts as you see them. You will need to rely on your experience, tied to the facts, to explain your rationale for your answering the question.

- **Me question:** This type of question generally centers on the personal experience of the executive. For example, they say, "We tried that solution in our group before, and it didn't work." Again, resist the temptation to challenge someone's experience—you cannot. People's experience is their experience. Instead, focus on your experience or the experience of certain subject matter experts who may have had a different experience to explain the recommendation or process. Just as you cannot challenge their experience, they really cannot challenge your experience either.

- **Paraphrase if necessary:** If you are not certain, use the technique of paraphrasing for clarity. Put the question into your own words, and they will tell you whether you are correct, or they will provide additional information for any part they believe you have misunderstood.

To recap, first be certain to assess the type of question you are hearing, and then respond in the appropriate way. If you answer a direct question with a personal experience answer, the impression you leave with the executive is that you are either avoiding the answer or do not know the answer. If you handle the questions correctly, you will have left a very positive impression on the executives you are working with.

Finally, one of the most difficult questions will begin with "why."

"Why do you believe this?" "Why did you assess the risks in that particular way?" For these types of questions, I have utilized a simple acronym to help me answer: REP:

- Reason or rationale for answering the why question
- Example or evidence that supports the reason
- Point that is your logical conclusion

When you finish your answer, confirm that the person who asked it feels you have responded. Realize he may not agree with your reason or example, but you have given an answer he can consider.

To review, these are the points to remember in getting help from your sponsor in dealing with cross-functional issues or problems.

- Use the technique of root cause analysis to help define the problem and gather the data.
- Ensure that there is clarity about the purpose of the decision that must be made.
- Review all the options considered and who worked on assessing the options.
- Make the executives aware of the time sensitivity in an attempt to create a sense of urgency.
- Plan with your sponsor who and how the information will be presented.
- Handle questions effectively by first assessing the type of question before answering.

Points to Remember

- Use root cause analysis.
- Use the escalation process to achieve resolution.
- Be sure to let your sponsor know about any time sensitivity.
- Prepare to present the information carefully.
- Provide answers based on the type of question asked.

20

Navigating the Political Waters

IN THIS CHAPTER, I want to cover how to work with your sponsor and other senior management and then move on to some of the negative aspects of company politics. In my experience talking to many project managers, the political landscape is one of the most frustrating aspects to deal with. I think part of the frustration stems from a lack of understanding of what is really going on, particularly as related to decisions made and actions taken.

The political landscape in most companies starts with the organization chart. The org chart defines who reports to whom and defines the relationships among people at a given time. However, that is only part of the story. The second half of the politics often relates to the individuals who occupy the positions on the org chart. This is where the informal hierarchy is established and affects who has access to information and when.

For example, in some companies I have worked with, the senior executive who oversees human resources is a very influential person in the decisions made by the CEO. In other companies I have worked with, the person in the same position is treated as if his presence is tolerated given the actions I have seen from others who would be equals on the org chart. So what is the difference, and how can a project manager use that to her advantage?

Trusted Advisor

The key to understanding the difference just described can be understood if you look at the concept of trusted advisor. If a person is seen as a trusted advisor, a key decision maker (in our case, the sponsor) turns to that person when seeking advice on solving a business problem. That is a different role from being an expert—in our case, an expert in managing projects. So let's review the difference between an expert and a trusted advisor.

> *Merriam-Webster's* defines trust as a "firm belief in the reliability, ability, or strength of someone."

It may appear to be a cliché, but a project manager's relationship with the sponsor and with other senior stakeholders is built on trust. Trust is absolutely essential. That is one reason I continue to reiterate the point that you must never let your sponsor be surprised. If he ever is surprised, his trust in you is weakened, and he will begin to be on guard in dealing with you about the project.

Building Blocks of Trust

The building blocks of trust are built on four conditions:

1. **Credibility:** "I believe what you say,"
2. **Reliability:** "I can depend on you,"

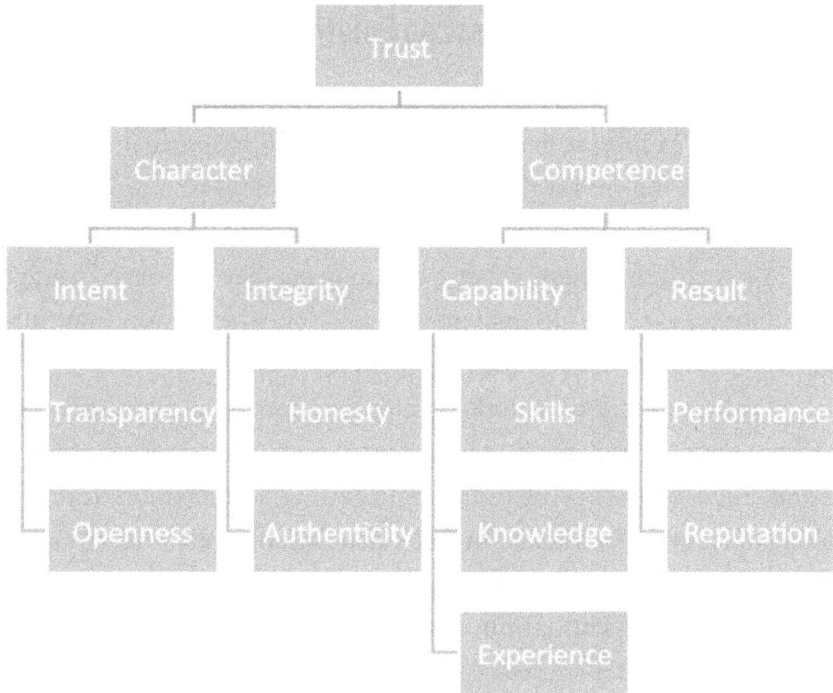

Figure 20.1: Building Blocks of Trust *Source: Adapted from Reyes Velasco.*

3. **Confidence:** "I feel comfortable in discussing this with you,"
4. **Personal Integrity:** "I have confidence that you are honest and have moral principles."

These four building blocks rest on a foundation, as illustrated in Figure 20.1. While all of these elements are important, my experience has taught me that transparency and performance are the two essentials for becoming a trusted advisor.

Emphasis on Solutions

A sponsor will begin to trust a project manager when the emphasis is on solutions. While we may need our sponsor's assistance in solving a problem, it is important that we come in with not just a problem but with a proposed solution that the sponsor can actually help with. And it is important to remember that our sponsor may not have leverage over another executive to implement a solution. The sponsor may only be in a position to request the help of another executive.

As an example, I was working a project for the vice president of technology. Our project affected the company's operations all over the world, and we were having difficulty in getting participation from one of the offices in Asia Pacific. In this situation, we knew what the solution was, but we needed the regional president to instruct his people to participate. In this situation, the regional president outranked my sponsor. This was a situation where company politics based on the organizational chart influenced what we could and could not accomplish. For reasons that even my sponsor never fully understood, the regional president felt that his operational goals took higher priority in his region, and he was willing to sacrifice the project implementation. In this project, our rollout was not as successful in that region. However, my sponsor was able to blunt criticism of the project with a detailed account of what we had requested, why we had requested these actions, and the response we received.

Keep the Business Goals Front and Center

Back in Chapter 1, I explained the process utilized, at a high level, that sanctions our projects. The project's approval means the management team decided to wager the company's money on achieving a business goal. Sometimes in a project with a long duration, the business climate or situation can change. We must always be mindful of that and make adjustments to the project to account for those changes. Nevertheless, don't attempt to make these changes without thorough consultation with the sponsor. Often the sponsor has additional information that we have not been privy to know. Just asking the question and seeking guidance gives the sponsor confidence and boosts your profile as a trusted advisor.

Receiving Top Cover

I worked for many years with project managers who were Air Force veterans and described the protection they received from their sponsor as "top cover." It was a term used in the Air Force to describe how aircraft were used to protect the infantry on the ground during combat. I think "top cover" is an appropriate term for the type of support we are looking for from our sponsor.

In my experience, the sponsor can provide top cover if you have worked with him as suggested in this book. The strategies and tactics I have outlined have allowed me to receive that kind of support. It also means being a trusted advisor on the project.

Having said that, even a great sponsor cannot avoid some aspects of projects. For example, I was doing a project for the chief technology officer of the company. The project was related to processes and procedures regarding how projects were sanctioned and implemented. I thought there could not be a better sponsor than someone from the C-suite. However, he has a boss too. About two months into the project, the CEO came to my sponsor and demanded a budget cut for all projects. Unfortunately, since this was the technology department, and my project was not related to actual technology, it was cancelled along with some others that did not make the priority list.

Negative Aspects of Company Politics

Unfortunately, we need to guard ourselves and our projects from the negative aspects of company politics as much as possible. These types of aspects are also referred to as hidden agendas. Some negative aspects are:

- Rumors.
- Games.
- Manipulation.
- Alliances.

Let's take a look at each of them, and I will try to give you advice based on my experience.

Rumors

We tend to think of rumors and gossip about others and their personal or private affairs. That is certainly true. However, some people use rumors to discredit a project, its sponsor, and its project manager. The reasons vary, but it usually involves people who believe that rumors can help them meet their personal goals for advancement at the expense of others.

If you think about the environment mentioned in the very first chapter, remember that at the executive level, these people sit at the top of a large pyramid. Just because they made it to the C-suite does not mean they have lost their ambition. Individuals may be competing with your sponsor, for example, to replace the CEO who is due to retire in the next three years, and people might be already positioning themselves to make a run at the position.

I have found that the best way to combat gossip and rumors is to have a strong and correctly targeted communication plan. It is very difficult for individuals to cast doubt on what is or is not happening in the project if the people who count are well-informed.

I would also suggest that you have a good network in place to provide feedback on any gossip that might be circulating. Address those rumors immediately, and try to pinpoint the source of the gossip. I would also recommend you inform your sponsor if you find the source. That information is useful to your sponsor because the person who began the rumor may not have been the actual source and may have been just passing on "information" heard from the executive boss. Recognizing the source can help your sponsor to be guarded in dealing with the other executive.

Games

To understand this type of office politics, think of it as a series of games. The place to start is to attempt to understand the perceived payoff. Project managers are sometimes guilty of games. An example of that game might be characterized as the No Bad News game. The project manager does not want the sponsor to get upset, so she suppresses any negative news about the project. Of course, sometimes that works, and things get sorted out before the sponsor becomes aware of problems. Usually, however, things continue to be negative, and the project manager has now damaged the trust the sponsor has in her.

Other games may be related to the changes your project is bringing to the company after implementation. Often, those who were responsible for the legacy system, process, or procedure are not happy, and they resist the new way of working. This executive may start playing games because he feels it threatens his power base within the company. In this situation, having a strong, comprehensive change management plan is essential. A change management plan that illustrates the benefits to the individuals involved in the work, including a strong training component, can overcome the game.

Manipulation

Often at the root of office politics is manipulation. In this case, others are determined to undermine the project. An example is where an executive has promised to provide technical resources to your project team but does nothing to create space in the person's workday to allow that participation. Some dedicated individuals will attempt to work two jobs—their day job and the project work—but make no mistake, a person's day-job responsibilities will always trump any promised work on the project. Again, look for the potential payback the manipulation might bring. You and your sponsor need to put together a strategy to end this behavior, and then you need to track the mitigation approach in your risk register.

Alliances

In any organization—and companies are no exception—natural alliances occur. One of the strongest ways to combat the politics is to observe who is in an alliance with your executive sponsor. You may or may not want to actually discuss this aspect until you have become a trusted advisor. However, you can carefully observe and listen to your sponsor as he discusses other members of the management team.

You will begin to pick up on whom your sponsor admires and who admires him. These alliances can be very important in dealing with the other negative aspects I have discussed. In a project I was leading where politics were particularly brutal, I uncovered the alliances my sponsor had forged—and those executives that he was not fond of. My sponsor and I built a very comprehensive engagement plan for those allies and a different but still robust communication plan for the antagonists. It worked, and my sponsor later ended up as CEO of the company.

Points to Remember

- Work very hard to become a trusted advisor.
- Maintain an emphasis on solutions.
- Keep the business goals front and center at all times.
- Be vigilant for office politics, and have a plan for mitigating those risks.

21

Engaging Senior Managers When You Have a Multinational, Cross-Cultural Project

IN DISCUSSING HOW to work with your sponsor and other executives on a multinational, multicultural project, let me first explain that I am coming from the perspective of a person from North America in general and from the United States in particular. While I lived in Toronto, Canada, most of my projects were initiated and managed from the United States. Therefore, when I suggest certain ideas or concepts, and you recognize that they may not work in your country, I would fully expect that. I would ask you to take the suggestions I am making and use your personal and professional judgment and experience to adjust accordingly.

Common Language for Business: English

I feel very fortunate that the universal language for business is English. As a result, professionals that I have worked with across the globe are very fluent in English—both speaking and writing it. So while that makes for certainty in many ways, it also should cause you to be aware of assumptions that you may be making that might not be true.

I have done several projects in the United Kingdom, where the native language of all involved is English. However, the assumption that all of us should understand one another can be misleading. A common example that I use to illustrate the point is the use of the word "boot." I was in the company headquarters in Houston, Texas, and when someone in Houston used the term "boot," it was almost certainly referring to footwear. However, if my colleagues in the UK were to use the same term in conversation, they were most likely referring to the storage space located in the rear of their personal automobile.

Now imagine a situation where the project team is composed of individuals from multiple countries, and English is a second language for many of them. The potential for misunderstandings or misquotes is much higher.

In these projects, I work very hard to explain the risks involved and to collaborate with my sponsor to secure the services of a communications specialist for the project. I truly believe that having an individual who is fluent in English and the dominant native language of the largest number of the project team is the best way to ensure successful communications.

My most important data in support of my request came from a survey I did for the world's largest oil field services company. The goal of the survey was to discover the best way to predict a successful project. Therefore, I asked project managers from all over the world to give me their answer to the question: "How can you predict a successful project?" I admit my bias going into the survey led me to believe I would receive answers such as:

- Good scope definition.
- Clear business objectives.
- Comprehensive contract and Statement of Work.

I did not get those as the most important factors (they were important, just not the primary factors). The most important factor cited by nearly three-quarters of the project managers was effective communications. If communications were strong among team members and between the project team and the customer (remember these were oil field services people), then the project would almost certainly be a success. If either or both of these communication channels were weak, the project would also certainly have problems.

Power Base

Sensitivity to the power base in multinational, multicultural projects is a critical requirement. You need to work closely with your sponsor to understand the protocol required within the various nationalities and cultures you are interacting with as part of the project.

Although I talked about the two sources of power earlier, authority and expertise, you must recognize that in many cultures, authority is the paramount source of power. In some of the projects I have managed, it would have been absolutely a cultural faux pas for me to talk to any senior manager within the stakeholder group. They would have spoken only to my sponsor based on the line of authority. Expertise is a distant second in those cultures.

I discussed the use of the RAPID method in Chapter 14 for decision making related to scope change. However, I believe expanding the areas of discussion with your sponsor is just as important. Why? Because the decisions and communications in a cross-cultural, multinational project have the political ramifications we looked at earlier, but the politics are played out within the culture context.

However, I fully recognize that it is often difficult to get the face time you need with a sponsor, particularly as you move into the execution phase. To handle that situation, I work with my sponsor to identify a champion. In a champion, I am seeking an individual who is well-known and well respected within the broad stakeholder network. I need my sponsor to help me in:

1. Finding the right person to fill the role
2. Negotiating this person's participation in the project with the executive the champion reports to

I am constantly using this person to prevent unforeseen misinterpretations of my communications or misunderstandings of my actions. She may also help with a feedback loop to stay in touch with the discussions on the ground, which harkens back to the warnings about rumors and gossip.

I will often include the champion in strategy meetings with the sponsor with a clear role of keeping me and the sponsor out of political trouble. I do not usually include them in standard status meetings.

Other Macro Barriers

In addition to language and culture, other potential barriers are involved in managing these complex projects. One of those factors may involve the workweek and national holidays.

In one project I managed, the team was divided into three locations: the United States, France, and the Middle East. So this project had people working nearly every day but not all the same days. It became tricky in scheduling meetings. Given the wide variations caused by time zones, I had to get my sponsor to help me understand the expectations in these countries about work meetings being held outside the normal business hours in that location. In France, for example, there are very strict laws about what work or other actions (like attending a meeting) an employer may ask of an employee outside the normal business day. As might be apparent, the team members in the United States always experienced the most inconvenient times to accommodate their colleagues overseas. My sponsor and I made gestures of thanks (e.g., catering breakfast or lunch and acknowledgment by the sponsor during staff meetings) to those people in order to recognize the sacrifice they were making by working extra and/or off-hours.

Jargon and Acronyms

Every company I have ever worked for has its own unique language. Often, even individual departments actually have their own shorthand as well. Many times, deciphering jargon and acronyms is the hardest thing for a new person to accomplish. In addition, it is also difficult for people from other countries and those for whom English is a second language.

I am not certain you can eliminate the practice, but you can make the situation better. I will circulate among key stakeholders to understand the jargon and acronyms they use on a regular basis. From that, I develop a Definitions Page as a reference guide for people on the project. However, before I publish the Definitions Page, I review it with my sponsor. Interestingly enough, I have actually found that sponsors are sometimes quite keen on eliminating the use of certain jargon and acronyms. They all have their own reasons for that, but that is why I always get approval before I publish it.

Human Resources

It is always wise to confer with your sponsor about national and regional laws you may need to comply with during the course of your project. Your sponsor may have you work with human resources to fully understand all of the aspects you must recognize. For example, if you are going to visit a location where some of the work is being completed, will you require a visa? In some countries, if you are just attending meetings, no visa is required. However, if you intend to stay for a couple of weeks and actually do work on the project, that same country may require a work visa.

I led a project in Norway, where the laws are very strict about when people are required to start and when they must be allowed to go home. In fact, I learned that if I needed to stay in the building after 6:00 p.m., I needed special permission!

Sensitivities

You must consider a multitude of sensitivities when working a multi-national, multicultural project, but discuss any possible issues with your sponsor. Most of the time, the sponsor has been in these countries and can give you good advice about what you should and should not do.

> **Empathy is the ability to understand and share the feelings of another.**
> *Paraphrased from Merriam-Webster*

Don't be like one project manager I heard about and be completely insensitive. The project manager had invited the entire team to a kick off dinner to celebrate the start of the project. He chose the best restaurant in town, which happened to be a steakhouse. The problem was that some of the team members were from India and followed the Hindu culture where cows are considered sacred animals. Unfortunately, the kickoff did not have the desired effect because the Indians would not attend.

I am guessing the sponsor could have enlightened the project manager had he asked where to hold the kickoff dinner. Particularly unfortunate was the blowback from that incident lasted for months.

Points to Remember

- Although English is the common language for business, be vigilant that people have a common understanding of the work.
- Work with your sponsor to determine the power base that will best meet your needs in overseas locations.
- Collaborate with your sponsor to understand the protocol you must follow in certain cultures or countries.
- Remain vigilant to other macro barriers that may impact your project.
- Beware of jargon and acronyms when working with people in other countries or cultures.
- Work with your sponsor and human resources to ensure your project is following all the laws and regulations in countries hosting the people working on the project.
- Remain sensitive to other cultural and religious practices that may be different from those you are familiar with.

22

Handling Competition
with Other Initiatives

EVERY PROJECT MANAGER has probably faced the time when their project was suddenly and unexpectedly impacted by other initiatives going on in the company at the same time. The frustration can mount when your project people are pulled away, causing a slippage in your schedule, and when that same program also diverts attention from your very important work. These circumstances may impact the:

- Availability of project team members.
- The political climate where all projects live.
- Accessibility to other people as the business prepares for the project deliverables.

The sense of being orphaned without management support or even interest can cause severe morale problems. Using your sponsor is a critical success factor in managing the competition from other initiatives.

The good news is that by combining the right engagement with your sponsor and appropriate communications, you can alleviate that situation to keep your project front and center with senior management. And you can minimize the negative influence on your project.

All project managers must adhere to some key principles if they are to be successful in managing internal competition:

1. Maintain situational awareness (defined as the awareness of other initiatives that may create potential conflicts over priorities and resources that impact the success of the project).
2. Plan communications that are horizontal as well as vertical.
3. Address potential conflicts quickly.

Maintain Situational Awareness

Project managers must pay particular attention to other initiatives going on within the business during the project. Many businesses will suffer from "initiative fatigue" because of the large number of projects going on at the same time. And they are very often not linked together very well. As a result, people feel overwhelmed by the sheer volume of work and changes they are asked to assume.

The other important consideration in awareness is to discuss these types of potential risks when you are meeting with your sponsor on the status of your project. I make it a point of asking my sponsor about particular initiatives that I believe may impact my project—particularly in a negative way.

I am always surprised that my sponsor may be in possession of important information about these other initiatives but does not think to tell me unless I specifically ask. I believe that, because of the large number of responsibilities my sponsor has in running the business, she has just not made the connection until I bring it up.

Also, I make it a point of trying to develop relationships with project managers who are leading these other initiatives. That usually entails inviting them to lunch every month or two to swap stories and chat about issues and get suggestions. However, the main purpose of the lunch, for me, is to find out whether any of these issues are going to affect my project. My attitude is that I cannot expect my sponsor to stay attuned to the interference of other initiatives if I am not doing my part.

I also make sure I am executing my communication plan for senior management. You might well ask, "How can communications help that situation?" In truth, I will not change the situation by communications. However, I can keep my project within senior management's consciousness by faithfully executing my communications plan, including continually reinforcing the Case for Change. I will also make adjustments to the communication plan when I believe that other initiatives might start to get in the way of my project's success, particularly as it relates to the schedule.

For example, I had a project to implement a new inventory management system that included making process changes in the shipping department. As you might have guessed, one of the major activities, as we worked to implement the system, required training the people in the shipping department. We had to train them on the new system and the use of the system within the new work processes. While we were executing the plan and preparing for go-live, I had to monitor another project that was under way to expand the shipping facilities. My concern was that training requirements might be related to the new facility as well as to my training on the new system. I collaborated with my sponsor to ensure that I could keep my schedule intact, including the training activity. My concern was that most organizations will not be receptive to taking their key personnel off the job for extended periods of training regardless of the importance and requirements.

In working with my sponsor and other executives, I must

understand how the initiatives fit together and whether there are any potential impacts to the critical path for my project and adjust accordingly. This happens very often when the project resource structure has project team members seconded from the business in a matrix structure. The operational responsibilities for these seconded team members will always take precedent over the work they are assigned for the project. Also, the best individuals will often be seconded to more than one initiative because they are the best! You may have to help them manage their bosses. They must balance priorities, and the answer cannot always be that my project is priority number one. If I attempt that strategy, I will lose any credibility with the team members and their supervisors.

In this situation, you may also need the help of your sponsor. If the sponsor does not have line authority over certain key individuals, he will need to negotiate to maintain his level of participation in the project. To do that, you must provide your sponsor with fairly detailed information on the nature of the work and why this individual's contribution and expertise are so critical to reaching the business goals. Frame the discussion in terms of business goals, not the project needs. The supervisors for these key resources may not feel a strong need to support the project unless they are aware of how their lack of participation hurts the business. This detailed information will also be helpful to your sponsor if he must go over the head of the supervisor and negotiate with another executive.

> **The key point to bear in mind about [political] influence is that it is often an informal method of power and control. Project managers who use influence well in furthering the goals of their projects usually work behind the scenes, negotiating, cutting deals, or collecting or offering IOUs.**
>
> *Jeffrey K. Pinto*[1]

In building your communication plan, always keep in mind the relationships of these multiple layers of leadership and management within the business. That will help you populate some of the sensitivities required, such as initiatives or projects affecting their departments. Also, be sensitive to the boundaries of their authority so that you do not inadvertently communicate in a way that shows you do not understand those boundaries. An example might be to ask a group of managers to manage certain aspects of an initiative or project that is important to your success but that is clearly beyond their ability to actually perform. A mistake like that will cause them to discount any information they receive from you from that point forward. They will be left with the impression, quite rightly, that you don't understand their situation.

Address Potential Conflicts Quickly

When potential conflicts arise between your project and another one, do not ignore them in the hope they will go away. Also remember to inform your sponsor about the potential conflict—no surprises! As you prepare to address the issue, you have to assess:

- Responsibility.
- Authority.
- Accountability.

Responsibility

You will need to be very clear about who is responsible for the situation and begin the exchange of ideas. This is the person you will need to work with to (hopefully) resolve the situation. Look for the minimum requirements you have for the situation, and be prepared to negotiate within those conditions should the need arise. Be sure to review your assessment of responsibility with the sponsor to ensure they agree you are working the problem correctly.

Authority

In some situations, you will not be able to successfully negotiate a solution and you will need to determine who has the authority to make a decision that both you and the other party can live with after it is made. That is the time to get your sponsor involved and lay out a strategy to resolve the issue at a higher level.

Political Climate

When you are communicating with others about the potential for a negative impact between projects, always consider the political situation before you act. Keep in mind that whether the message is written on paper or as part of an e-mail, it tends to be seen by others for a variety of reasons. Always keep in mind those "secondary readers."

> **Secondary readers are people for whom the message was not intended (the primary reader) but who have come into possession of that e-mail and might have a strong response to its content.**

How would secondary readers receive the information and react to it? And remember, for situations of a political nature, keep those messages brief and to the point. Be careful and make each message count. If you are ever in doubt about the wisdom of a written note, then do not send it before conferring with your sponsor, if possible. Better to call someone on the telephone or meet in person. A face-to-face meeting allows for plausible deniability.

Most successful business people have a keen sense of what is appropriate when talking to others, but many fail to apply this judgment to their writing. Often their writing is far too stiff and formal or too relaxed and colloquial. For an appropriate tone, you need to monitor two attributes of your writing—the degree of motivation required and level of formality.

Richard Bierck[2]

Points to Remember

- Recognize that your project is not the only initiative going on in the company and that you will need to monitor other initiatives for their impact on your project.
- Maintain situational awareness.
- Handle conflicts quickly and use techniques as required to address those conflicts.

If you follow the guidelines in this chapter and keep an eye on other projects vying for attention, you will keep your project front and center with senior management, and you will receive the support you need to be successful.

NOTES

CHAPTER 7

1 Kittie Watson and Larry Barker, *Listen Up!* (St. Martin's Press, 2000).

CHAPTER 8

1 Charles R. Swindoll, *Great Attitudes for Graduates! 10 Choices for Success in Life* (J. Countryman, 2006).

CHAPTER 10

1 Adapted from Vijay Verma, *Human Resource Skills for the Project Manager* (Project Management Institute, 1996).

CHAPTER 14

1 SAP is a common ERP in North America and Europe.

CHAPTER 17

1 Hans Finzel, *The Top Ten Mistakes Leaders Make* (Cook Communications, 1994).

CHAPTER 22

1 Jeffery K Pinto, *Power and Politics in Project Management* (Project Management Institute, 1998), p. 260.

2 Richard Bierck, *Find the Right Tone for Your Business Writing: Written Communications That Influence and Inform* (Harvard Business School Press, 2006), p. 86.

INDEX